A Better Beginning

Supporting and Mentoring New Teachers

EDITED BY MARGE SCHERER

Association for Supervision
and Curriculum Development
Alexandria, Virginia USA

Association for Supervision and Curriculum Development
1703 N. Beauregard St. • Alexandria, VA 22311-1714 USA
Telephone: 1-800-933-2723 or 703-578-9600 • Fax: 703-575-5400
Web site: http://www.ascd.org • E-mail: member@ascd.org

Printed in the United States of America.
s11/99
ASCD Stock No. 199236
ASCD member price: $21.95 nonmember price: $25.95

Library of Congress Cataloging-in-Publication Data

A better beginning : supporting and mentoring new teachers / edited by Marge Scherer.
p. cm.
"ASCD Stock No. 199236."
Includes bibliographical references and index.
ISBN 0-87120-355-3 (pbk. : alk. paper)
I. Scherer, Marge, 1945- 1. First year teachers—United States. 2. Mentoring in education—United States.
LB2844.1.N4 B48 1999
371.1—dc21
99-006859

08 07 06 05 04 03 10 9 8 7 6 5 4 3

A Better Beginning

Supporting and Mentoring New Teachers

Part III. Making Mentoring Meaningful

Part IV. Planning Comprehensive Teacher Support

Part V. Improving Instruction and Communication

Part VI. Listening to Teachers

A New Teacher's World: Not Your Grandmother's Classroom

Marge Scherer

Scott Lane Elementary School has been generating stories in *The San Jose Mercury News* for two years now. This Silicon Valley school has embarked on a mission that the media are intensely interested in following.

> Scott Lane Elementary has made a promise to 115 kindergartners: We'll teach you to read fluently by the end of second grade. If your family's poor, we'll teach you to read. If you don't speak English very well, we'll teach you to read. If you show up in school not knowing the alphabet, not knowing how to write your own name, not knowing what a book looks like because nobody read stories to you, we'll teach you to read. No excuses. (1997)

The "1,000 Day Pledge"—named for the approximate number of days the school has to make its promise good—comes with many challenges. Many of the children enter school already far behind other kids their age. Sixty percent are poor enough to qualify for subsidized lunch, and 40 percent are immigrant children for whom English is not their first language. Although the media and the business community endorse the school's effort—and parents and volunteers are enlisted to help—the pressure to fulfill the promise that every 3rd grader will read at or above grade level rests primarily on the teachers. And that's where the story behind the story comes in.

Of the 32 teachers responsible to the school's kindergartners, and to the other 500 students in the school, more than half are new to the profession. Eighteen Scott Lane teachers have from zero to three years' experience in the classroom. Eight of them are filling new positions at the school; the additional number is necessitated by the state regulation that has reduced class size to 20 students.

Principal Steve Kay says, "We're drowning in good news. . . . Every state or federal mandate that allows us to tackle a needed reform comes with an accountability clause that exacerbates the need to find new teachers skilled enough to make a difference." Kay emphasizes the word *new*. "The baby boomers are out [of teaching], and the baby boomers' kids are in. Schools are experiencing a changing of the guard, but the issues that a new teacher faces now are quite different from those that new teachers faced in the 60s." He ticks off some significant changes: the increasing diversity of students; a complex new technology to learn and teach; a more pronounced accountability demanded of schools by businesses, media, and governments; and higher expectations from parents.

Scott Lane Elementary School is not unlike other schools in facing such challenges, and it is not unlike others in competing for new teachers. Because a growing number of children are entering our schools, because retirements of many experienced teachers are imminent, and because the high drop-out rate among new teachers continues, many more beginning teachers will staff our schools in the next decade. The majority of the newcomers will fit the profile of a white, female teacher in her 20s with less than three years of experience. The new teachers will enter the profession with varying levels of preparation—some with emergency certificates; some with a little background in education; others with a thorough grounding in both academics and field experience (Futrell, 1999).

In some regions, the demand for new teachers is already outpacing the supply. In some states, colleges and universities can certify only a small portion of the new teachers needed each year. Many districts must recruit candidates from other regions. Despite unfamiliar surroundings and with much to learn about their new students and profession, new teachers who are eager to teach are accepting the opportunity. Most embark on their journey with a great deal of enthusiasm, for, unlike in the past when there were fewer job opportunities for women, teaching is their *chosen* career.

If the beginners are fortunate, they will find themselves in a school like Scott Lane where along with the challenges will come support. For example, Scott Lane provides all teachers a literacy education course that starts in the summer and continues during the school year. The class familiarizes teachers with research and gives them time to practice new reading strategies. During the school year, a master mentor is available every day to offer just-in-time staff development. A new teacher can request help or advice inside or outside the classroom and receive assistance by the next day, whether the problem concerns a student, classroom management, or instruction.

To strengthen relationships among colleagues, teachers are furnished e-mail access at home so that in the evenings when many do their preparations or reflect on their day, they can contact one another. And the administration tries to make evaluation an opportunity for learning, too. After the principal videotapes a teacher's lesson, he hands it to the teacher when he leaves the classroom. At appraisal time, the teacher may bring the tape back, cuing the tape at several places he or she has chosen to open the discussion about strengths and weaknesses.

Thus, this school tries to go "beyond support" of its newest staff toward offering career-long professional development to them—a concept that Sharon Feiman-Nemser and her colleagues propose in Part I of this book. The idea, as these authors explain it, is to "take new teachers seriously as learners" so that they can meet the enormous challenges ahead. Contrast this with the old days when most new teachers were on their own behind closed doors with the toughest classes the school could offer.

"It is an interesting time to be a new teacher," Principal Steve Kay noted on a visit to the ASCD offices while we were working on this book. "The classroom of the next century will be a whole new world."

This book, *A Better Beginning: Supporting and Mentoring New Teachers*, written by educators who are revitalizing the profession from within, investigates how to keep new teachers and help them thrive.

Perhaps it is time to make a 1,000-day pledge to our youngest colleagues: "We will support you as you begin your journey toward being a master teacher. No excuses."

References

Futrell, M. H. (1999, May). Recruiting minority teachers. *Educational Leadership*, 56, 30–33.

Spelling out commitment: Scott Lane School's reading promise should be the norm, not a news story. (1997, December 2). *The San Jose Mercury News*, p. 6B.

Marge Scherer, editor, *Educational Leadership*, ASCD, 1703 N. Beauregard St., Alexandria, VA 22311-1714. (e-mail: el@ascd.org)

About This Book

This book, *A Better Beginning: Supporting and Mentoring New Teachers*, began as an outgrowth of a theme issue of *Educational Leadership* ("Supporting New Teachers," May 1999). Realizing that we had a wealth of articles written by authors steeped in these issues, the editors of *Educational Leadership* compiled this anthology. It documents how schools and educators are responding to the needs of new teachers. The six sections reflect trends in the profession to examine the needs of new teachers (Part I); and to provide better induction (Part II); improved mentoring (Part III); comprehensive reforms (Part IV); stronger communication and instructional competencies (Part V); and more attention to fellow practitioners (Part VI).

In Part I, "What Do New Teachers Need?" the authors establish the reasons for stepping up the quality and quantity of support programs for novices. They report on the extent of the retention and attrition problems and provide compelling reasons why it is necessary, as Sharon Feiman-Nemser and her colleagues urge, to go beyond providing beginners psychological support and begin to honor new teachers as learners. Ellen Moir, a director of a New Teacher Center, ends this section by tracing the stages that new teachers experience during their first year of teaching.

In Part II, "Creating an Induction Program," educators who have designed successful induction programs to help novices get off to a better start share lessons learned. Authors describe summer programs, five-day programs, and yearlong orientations for high schools and elementary schools in private and public settings in states as diverse as Louisiana and Minnesota.

Part III, "Making Mentoring Meaningful," gives readers a sampling of the multitude of mentoring programs being instituted in schools across the country. As this book goes to press, 28 states and the District of Columbia have piloted some form of mentoring program, although funding levels and number of teachers served differ greatly. These articles give specific ideas about how to shape the delicate, dynamic relationship between newcomers and their mentors. Several of the authors of this section are site coordinators of mentoring programs, and several are classroom teachers who have had personal experience as mentors. They share their philosophy as well as their know-how as they describe how to make mentoring relationships result in better teaching for all participants.

Part IV, "Planning Comprehensive Teacher Support," looks at the systemic reforms that incorporate induction, mentoring, assessment, and professional development. Several articles feature California, a bellwether state for mentoring policy. Others describe model district programs. Authors document the elements of the programs that yield positive results and explain the process of putting together mentoring programs that comply with state and district professional teaching standards.

In Part V, "Improving Instruction and Communication," authors address how to expand a new teacher's repertoire of effective teaching strategies. For example, Jeffrey Frykholm and Margaret R. Meyer (p. 145) detail a model that unites key players in teacher preparation—university, school, and student teacher—in an effort to encourage innovative teaching. Paul Caccia (p. 157) explains "linguistic coaching," a way of holding conversations about teaching that helps veterans and their younger colleagues learn together.

In the final section, "Listening to Teachers," teachers and teachers of teachers write their perspectives on what newcomers need. For example, Beth Hurst and Ginny Reding, self-described as "teachers who still love to teach," share their insights about maintaining the optimistic outlook needed by all who work with children and adolescents. The final essay by Lisa Renard begins with a case study of a teacher who gets off to a rocky start but who salvages the situation. Her motto: "Ask not what your school can do for you, but what *you* can do for you."

A Better Beginning: Supporting and Mentoring New Teachers is dedicated to all those in the teaching profession—those who are starting out and those who are staying in—who are striving to create teaching conditions where good teachers thrive—and who are willing to support their professional colleagues along the way.

PART I

WHAT DO NEW TEACHERS NEED?

Beyond Support: Taking New Teachers Seriously As Learners

Sharon Feiman-Nemser, Cynthia Carver, Sharon Schwille, and Brian Yusko

Support is essential to retaining new teachers, but the ultimate goal of beginning-teacher induction must be the development of professionals who can help complex learning happen for students.

Although the idea of formal programs to assist beginning teachers is not new, the movement to establish such programs has gained considerable momentum since the mid-1980s. Before 1980, only one state had mandated an induction program. Since then, the scale of induction activity has increased dramatically. Today, more states are mandating induction programs than ever before, and more urban districts offer some kind of support to beginning teachers, usually in the form of mentoring (Fideler & Haselkorn, in press).

Beginning-teacher induction has broad-based support. High attrition rates during the early years of teaching and serious teacher shortages make programs that improve teacher retention attractive. Stories about the trials and tribulations of new teachers lend weight to the idea of beginning-teacher support. The realization that new teachers, even those with good preservice preparation, are still learning to teach underscores the need for ongoing professional development. Finally, raised expectations for student achievement, combined with concerns about quality assurance, highlight the need to link beginning-teacher assistance with standards-based assessments.

Despite widespread interest and broad-based support, however, the overall picture is uneven. Most induction mandates do not rest on robust ideas about teacher learning, and they often lack the human resources and materials to support effective programs. Even when formal programs exist, they may not help beginning teachers learn the kind of teaching that fosters complex learning on the part of students. Research shows that mentoring, the most popular induction strategy, may perpetuate traditional norms and practices rather than promote high-quality teaching.

Linking Support and Assessment Through Learning

Education leaders must explore three concepts associated with beginning-teacher induction—support, development, and assessment. These concepts reflect some of the confusions and contradictions visible in current induction policies and practice. They also reflect shifting ideas about the purposes of programs for beginning teachers.

Much early thinking and practice put the emphasis squarely on assistance and support during the first year of teaching (Brooks, 1987; Huling-Austin, 1990). Recently, policy recommendations have centered on the role of assessment (National Commission on Teaching and America's Future, 1996; National Association of State Boards of Education, 1998). The link between support and assessment is teacher learning. If we want beginning-teacher induction to improve the quality of teaching and learning, we must move beyond a general recognition that new teachers need support to more powerful conceptions of induction as part of a broader system of professional development and accountability.

The Dominance of Support

Paired with assistance, the term *support* represents the dominant orientation and focus of most induction programs (Huling-Austin, 1990; Gold, 1996; Fideler & Haselkorn, in press). Support connotes a responsive stance toward beginning teachers whose problems, needs, and concerns justify the existence of mentor teachers and other support providers. Support is the omnibus term used to describe the materials, resources, advice, and hand-holding that mentors offer new teachers.

The challenges associated with the first year of teaching make the case for beginning-teacher support seem self-evident. Charged with the same responsibilities as their more experienced colleagues, new teachers are expected to perform and be effective. Yet most aspects of the situation are unfamiliar—the students, the curriculum, the community, and the local policies and procedures.

Besides the newness of the situation, the complexities of teaching itself confront the novice with daily dilemmas and uncertainties. With limited experience and practical knowledge to draw on, many beginning teachers feel overwhelmed and uncertain. On top of this, the isolation of teachers in their own classrooms and the prevailing norms of autonomy and noninterference make it difficult to ask for and receive help. To make matters even worse, beginning teachers often get the most difficult classes or teach subjects for which they have little or no preparation.

Clearly, providing support to beginning teachers is better than letting them sink or swim on their own. Studies of teacher attrition show that without support, new teachers are more likely to leave teaching, a burden that falls heaviest on urban schools (Darling-Hammond, 1997). Some evidence also shows that with support, new teachers move more quickly from concerns about management and control to concerns about instruction (Odell, 1986).

Still, the vagueness of the term leaves many questions unanswered. What assumptions about teaching and learning to teach inform the concept of support? How much and what kinds of support contribute to the well-being of new teachers and to the learning of their students? How does a discourse of support influence the way support providers think about their role?

Types of Support

In a review of the literature on beginning-teacher induction, Gold (1996) identifies two broad categories of support: (1) instruction-related support that includes "assisting the novice with the knowledge, skills, and strategies necessary to be successful in the classroom and school" and (2) psychological support aimed at "building the protégé's sense of self and ability to handle stress" (p. 561). She notes that the first category includes attention to subject-matter knowledge and the teaching and learning of specific subjects, topics that rarely surface in discussions of beginning-teacher support. She argues that the second category, which she defines as "a form of therapeutic guidance," is more important and should not be neglected.

Interpreting support as a psychological construct goes hand in hand with a tendency to orient induction activities, especially mentoring, around the self-defined needs, problems, and concerns of beginning teachers. For a skilled mentor, responding to immediate needs and concerns may be the starting point for joint work on teaching. Still, a discourse of support may persuade others, like the mentor teacher quoted below, that just being there and responding to requests for help is an end in itself.

> The mentor is supposed to just be there when you need her for whatever. They (the novice teachers) know that. . . . I establish that with them at the very beginning, that I'm here to help you in any capacity. What I do is make suggestions and I tell them, "If you don't follow them it's all right. Maybe what I suggest is something you feel that you can't use." (Feiman-Nemser & Parker, 1993, p. 699)

Offering support to new teachers is a humane response to the very real challenges of beginning teaching. Many new teachers testify that they could not have survived without the support and encouragement of their mentor teacher (Bartell & Ownby, 1994). Moreover, new teachers have different strengths and vulnerabilities, and different working conditions call for different forms of help and assistance. Unless we also take into account the fact that new teachers are learners, we may design programs that reduce stress and address immediate problems without promoting development. To improve the practice of beginning teachers and to foster a sense of collective responsibility for student learning, we need to move beyond psychological models of teacher concerns to consider the "what" and the "how" of beginning-teacher learning.

The Need for Development

Many people assume that once individuals complete their formal preparation for teaching, they are ready to teach on their own. This assumption is misleading. As Griffin (1987) writes:

> Although it is comforting to invest full confidence in the first-year teacher, this confidence is seldom warranted. Men and women new to teaching, although modestly familiar with the work of teaching, are still learning it. (p. v)

Beginning teachers have two jobs to do—they have to teach and they have to learn to teach. On their own, beginning teachers often develop "safe" practices that enable them to survive. Induction programs should help them develop "best" practices and become learners through their teaching.

If we took new teachers seriously as learners, we would not expect them to do the same job or have the same skills as experienced teachers. Rather, we would adjust our expectations for success and effectiveness to fit their career stage and structure their assignments to allow time for observation, coplanning, collaborative problem solving, and reflection.

Education leaders have put forward various proposals to differentiate the scope of teachers' professional activity and responsibility on the basis of their levels of knowledge and expertise (Holmes Group, 1987; Carnegie Forum on Education and the Economy, 1986). Most include recommendations about extended learning opportunities through internships and residencies before teachers become fully certified. For example, the National Commission on Teaching and America's Future (1996) recommends that the first two years of teaching be structured like a residency in medicine, with teachers regularly consulting an experienced teacher about the decisions they are making and receiving ongoing advice and feedback. Such policies and practices, visible in a handful of programs in the United States, treat new teachers like the novices and learners that they are.

Induction programs aimed at teacher development rest on a vision of good teaching and a consideration of what beginning teachers need to learn. Professional teaching standards, such as those developed by the Interstate New Teacher Assessment and Support Consortium (1996), can inform such thinking. By outlining the knowledge, dispositions, and skills that teachers need to promote ambitious learning for all students, these standards offer powerful goals for new-teacher development and a common language for talking about teaching. Helping new teachers figure out what professional standards mean and what they look like in practice is a central task of teacher induction.

Toward Powerful Teaching

The kind of teaching implied by new standards requires teachers to know their subjects deeply and represent them in authentic ways, to understand how students think about subject matter, and to promote critical thinking and active learning (Cohen, McLaughlin, & Talbert, 1993). One hallmark of this kind of teaching is its responsiveness to students' ideas. To teach in ways that extend student thinking, teachers must be able to gather information about students' ideas and ways of thinking and use that information to improve their instruction. And they must gather and use much of this information in classrooms as the lesson unfolds (Lampert, 1985).

In order to learn this kind of teaching, teachers need professional development connected to the daily work of students, related to the teaching and learning of subject matter, organized around real problems of practice, and sustained over time by conversation and coaching. Researchers and reform-minded educators are recommending the same kind of learning opportunities for all teachers (Little, 1993; Sparks, 1995; Darling-Hammond & McLaughlin, 1996). Induction programs that offer such opportunities to new teachers generally have a multiyear time frame, a developmental stance toward teacher learning, and a view of mentoring as a form of teaching.

Mentors who see their work in educational terms are well positioned to help new teachers get inside the intellectual and practical challenges of teaching for understanding. Clear about the need for support and development, they keep one eye on immediate concerns and one eye on long-term professional goals, such as helping new teachers pay attention to student thinking and develop sound reasons for their actions. They work toward these goals by inquiring with novices into the particulars of their practice, asking such questions as "What sense did students make of that assignment?" "Why did you decide on that activity?" and "How can we find out whether it was effective?" Like the mentor who said, "I see myself as a co-thinker trying to move my novices toward paths of growth" (Feiman-Nemser, 1992), they think about mentoring as a joint inquiry into teaching and learning.

The Role of Assessment

Many leaders in the induction movement believe that assistance and assessment are incompatible functions that should not be carried out in the same program (Huling-Austin, 1990). They argue that new teachers, eager to make a good impression, would be reluctant to share problems and ask for help if they had to worry about being evaluated. They also point out that high-stakes evaluation for purposes of licensing or continued employment is traditionally an administrative function.

This position has been challenged by those who view formative assessment as an integral part of teacher development and by others who believe that induction programs should play both a "bridging" and a "gatekeeping" function (Sweeney, 1998). The integration of assistance and assessment takes different forms in different programs. The alternatives suggest new directions for induction policy and practice.

Formative assessment is a central feature of California's Beginning Teacher Support and Assessment Program, which serves first- and second-year teachers who have completed preservice preparation. Support providers and beginning teachers work together to identify each new teacher's strengths and areas for growth through a formative-assessment process. Using assessment data, the support provider and beginning teacher develop an Individual Induction Plan, which identifies professional development activities to improve the new teacher's knowledge and practice. The California Standards for the Teaching Profession provide a framework for ongoing formative assessment and a common language for talking about teaching.

Connecticut's Beginning Educator Support and Training Program integrates assistance with formative and summative assessment, but different people provide the two kinds of assessment. All new teachers work with a school-based mentor or team who responds to their instructional and noninstructional needs and helps them prepare for assessments in their first and second year of teaching. First-year teachers participate in an assessment process that reflects Connecticut's "essential teaching competencies." Second-year teachers compile a teaching portfolio that is assessed by trained assessors using criteria from content-specific professional teaching standards. When beginning teachers meet the acceptable standard, they are recommended for provisional certification.

A third approach to the integration of assistance and assessment comes from peer assistance and review programs. Following the example of Toledo, Ohio, three additional cities—Cincinnati and Columbus, Ohio, and Rochester, New York—have negotiated induction programs in which veteran teachers, on leave for up to two years, provide assistance to beginning teachers and make recommendations about contract renewal. Supportive union leaders argue that educators should make decisions about who enters the teaching profession.

The sharp dichotomy between assistance and assessment seems shortsighted in the context of beginning-teacher induction. Thoughtful teachers use ongoing assessment to identify goals, provide feedback, and document progress. Similarly, new teachers and those responsible for their learning need a defensible basis for deciding what to work toward and some means of determining how they are doing. Formative assessment based on a shared vision of good teaching and clear goals for teacher learning provides purpose to induction activity.

Linking induction and high-stakes assessment in a responsible way is a different matter. Increased attention to standards and accountability for students has led to new performance assessments for beginning teachers. The danger is that states and districts may adopt new assessments and licensing standards without providing the resources to help new teachers learn to meet those standards in practice. Unless new teachers have opportunities for serious and sustained learning, high-stakes assessment will not lead to quality teaching.

The Key Is New-Teacher Development

Support. Development. Assessment. All three are necessary components in a comprehensive system of beginning-teacher induction. Support without development leaves teacher learning to chance. It favors the agendas of individual teachers and works against a sense of collective responsibility for student learning. Framing induction around new-teacher development closes the gap between initial preparation and continuing professional development. It honors the fact that new teachers are learners and lays a foundation for the ongoing study and improvement of teaching. Assessment that encourages interpretation and enactment of standards in context strengthens professional accountability, which is the most appropriate and powerful source of quality control in teaching.

References

Bartell, C., & Ownby, L. (1994). *Report on the implementation of the Beginning Teacher Support and Assessment Program, 1992–1994*. Sacramento, CA: California Commission on New Teacher Credentialing and California Department of Education.

Brooks, D. M. (Ed.). (1987). *Teacher induction: A new beginning*. Reston, VA: National Commission on the Teacher Induction Process, Association of Teacher Educators.

Carnegie Forum on Education and the Economy. (1986). *A nation prepared: Teachers for the 21st century*. Report of the Task Force on Teaching As a Profession. New York: Carnegie Corporation.

Cohen, D., McLaughlin, M., & Talbert, J. (1993). *Teaching for understanding*. San Francisco: Jossey-Bass.

Darling-Hammond, L. (1997). *Doing what matters most: Investing in quality teaching*. New York: National Commission on Teaching and America's Future.

Darling-Hammond, L., & McLaughlin, M. (1996). Policies that support teacher development in an era of reform. In M. McLaughlin & I. Oberman (Eds.), *Teacher learning: New policies and practices* (pp. 202–218). New York: Teachers College Press.

Feiman-Nemser, S. (1992). *Helping novices learn to teach: Lessons from an exemplary support teacher*. (Research Report 91-6). East Lansing, MI: National Center for Research on Teacher Learning, Michigan State University.

Feiman-Nemser, S., & Parker, M. (1993). Mentoring in context: A comparison of two U.S. programs for beginning teachers. *International Journal of Educational Research, 19*(8), 699–718.

Fideler, E., & Haselkorn, D. (in press). *Learning the ropes: Urban teacher induction programs and practices in the United States*. Belmont, MA: Recruiting New Teachers, Inc.

Gold, Y. (1996). Beginning teacher support: Attrition, mentoring and induction. In J. Sikula, T. J. Buttery, & E. Guyton (Eds.), *Handbook of research on teacher education* (pp. 548–594). New York: Macmillan.

Griffin, G. (1987). Foreword in G. Griffin & S. Millies (Eds.), *The first years of teaching: Background papers and a proposal*. Chicago: University of Illinois, Chicago.

Holmes Group. (1987). *Tomorrow's teachers: A report of the Holmes Group*. East Lansing, MI: Author.

Huling-Austin, L. (1990). Teacher induction programs and internships. In R. W. Houston (Ed.), *Handbook of research on teacher education* (pp. 535–548). New York: Macmillan.

Interstate New Teacher Assessment and Support Consortium. (1996). *INTASC fact sheet*. Washington, DC: Council of Chief State School Officers.

Lampert, M. (1985). How do teachers manage to teach? *Harvard Education Review, 55*(2), 178–194.

Little, J. W. (1993). Teachers' professional development in a climate of educational reform. *Educational Evaluation and Policy Analysis, 15*(2), 129–151.

National Association of State Boards of Education. (1998). *The numbers game: Ensuring quantity and quality in the teaching work force.* Alexandria, VA: Author.

National Commission on Teaching and America's Future. (1996). *What matters most: Teaching for America's future.* New York: Author.

Odell, S. J. (1986). Induction support of new teachers: A functional approach. *Journal of Teacher Education, 37*(1), 26–29.

Sparks, D. (1995). A paradigm shift in staff development. *The ERIC Review, 3*(3), 2–4.

Sweeney, B. A. (1998). *A survey of the 50 state-mandated novice teacher programs: Implications for state and local mentoring programs and practices.* [On-line]. Available: http://www.teachermentors.com

---

Sharon Feiman-Nemser (e-mail: snemser@pilot.msu.edu) is Professor of Teacher Education, **Cynthia Carver** is a doctoral student in teacher education, **Sharon Schwille** (e-mail: sharons@msu.edu) is Senior Academic Specialist in Teacher Education, and **Brian Yusko** is a doctoral student in teacher education at Michigan State University. The authors can be reached in care of Sharon Feiman-Nemser at Michigan State University, Erickson Hall, East Lansing, MI 48824.

Easing the Way for New Teachers

Joan Montgomery Halford

How can schools support novice educators so that they not only survive, but also thrive?

Julia Archer was elated when she accepted her first job teaching social studies at Whitman Middle School. She had just completed a graduate-level teacher preparation program at a prestigious university, and she was eager to make a difference with students as a permanent staff member.

Julia's first week, however, quickly dampened her enthusiasm. Although the principal held a brief orientation for new teachers, the meeting was a perfunctory overview of school procedures, not a chance to build a support network or discuss the school's vision. Julia then learned that she would have four different course preparations for her five classes—and that the classes had become "dumping grounds" for students with chronic behavior, attendance, and learning difficulties. Her new colleagues in the social studies department were friendly, but few had time to help Julia address the serious challenges in her classroom. As a new teacher, Julia also soon realized that she lacked an adequate repertoire of teaching strategies.

Nothing in her teacher preparation program, including her one-year internship at another school, had prepared Julia for the isolation she would experience during her first months at Whitman. As a new teacher in a probationary period, Julia was concerned that seeking assistance for her classroom problems would be viewed as a sign of incompetence. She also began to question whether her colleagues shared her philosophy of teaching and learning, and this compounded her concerns. As the school

---

Author's note: Julia Archer and Whitman Middle School are pseudonyms.
Editor's note: This article was originally published in *Educational Leadership*, February 1998.

year wore on, Julia wore out. Teaching left her with feelings of disillusionment and failure, shattering her idealism. By June, Julia decided to leave teaching and pursue another career.

The Profession That Eats Its Young

Julia's story encapsulates the thousands behind the staggering teacher attrition rate in the United States today. Nearly 30 percent of teachers leave in the first five years, and the exodus is even greater in some school districts. Further, research indicates that the most talented new educators are often the most likely to leave (Gonzales & Sosa, 1993). Given comparisons to fields such as medicine and law, which recognize the needs of new professionals more fully, some observers have dubbed education "the profession that eats its young."

Teacher turnover threatens school reform, which requires years of sustained staff effort. And even for teachers who remain in the classroom, difficulties in the formative professional years can have a continuing negative effect. "When we don't ease the way into schools, it's a signal about how people—including teachers, parents, and the kids—are valued," notes Mary E. Diez, director of the Master of Arts in Education program at Alverno College in Milwaukee, Wisconsin. Ultimately, students suffer the consequences of inadequate support for beginning teachers.

Nearly two million new teachers are projected to enter U.S. schools in the next decade, and the challenge of supporting them effectively has become a critical issue. "The demand for new teachers is a real concern—and an opportunity," says James Rowley, associate professor at the University of Dayton. "It's a chance to bring in fresh young minds." But recruiting talented, competent educators is only a first step; schools must also help novice teachers develop staying power. Linda Darling-Hammond, executive director of the National Commission on Teaching and America's Future, asserts, "To retain new teachers, we must do two things: design good schools in which to teach and employ mentoring."

Schools That View New Teachers As Learners

The need to design schools that are good places for educators, novice and experienced, is a perennial concern. In many cases, creating a positive induction experience for new teachers is an essential component of this reform. At the core of such support efforts is the recognition that all teachers, particularly new teachers, are learners. In addition to learning how to effectively work with a variety of students, new teachers are in the throes of developing a professional identity and navigating a new school culture. As Fuller's classic (1969) research suggests, new educators often progress through predictable, developmental stages of concern, gradually shifting from a primary focus on survival to a primary focus on student learning.

Education leaders who understand the typical realities of new teachers can anticipate and address the needs of these novices. Class assignments are a starting point. North Carolina Governor James B. Hunt Jr., chair of the National Commission on Teaching and America's Future, notes, "Teachers with the least training are assigned to teach the most disadvantaged students." Schools can often avoid setting beginning teachers up for failure by more carefully considering their teaching schedules.

Schools and universities are also seeking ways to build a better bridge from preservice preparation to the early years of teaching. Diez points out that beginning teachers often experience problems when the beliefs they developed during their university-based teacher preparation stand in contrast to the school culture they encounter in their first teaching assignments. "We need to work with new teachers to help them articulate their beliefs—not so they can be argumentative, but so they can advocate," she states. "New people need an orientation during which they can begin to discuss the vision and the mission of the school, not just 'here are the keys, here are the procedures.'" Recruiting practices that enable beginning teachers to consider the curricular approaches of individual schools are another way to ensure more appropriate teaching assignments for novices.

New teachers also benefit when universities work more closely with school districts. Although university faculty sometimes assist beginning teachers after preservice preparation, some school districts and universities are establishing more formal partnerships. Among these partnerships are collaborations that develop cadres of trained mentors to bolster beginning teachers.

Mentoring: Relationships to Grow On

From classrooms to commission chambers, education leaders are recognizing the power of mentoring. In California, a state study found that among the many approaches to supporting new teachers, the most effective focused on the relationship between the new teacher and a support provider (California Commission on Teacher Credentialing, 1992). "Simply put, new teachers need somebody to talk to," says Terry Janicki, consultant at the California Commission on Teacher Credentialing. As part of the California Beginning Teacher Support and Assessment (BSTA) program, the state recently earmarked $17 million toward mentors (technically called "support providers") for beginning teachers.

Support programs that focus on mentoring relationships have caught on at state and district levels nationwide. "The chance to connect to a veteran peer is a powerful resource," Rowley says. As instructional leaders and master teachers, mentors can be a professional lifeline for their new colleagues.

For Mindy Cline, a kindergarten teacher in Centerville, Ohio, mentor Barb Roberts smoothed the initial transition into teaching. From the mundane to the philosophical, Roberts lent a hand—and an ear—in Cline's new classroom. She helped Cline arrange her room, reviewed her early lesson plans, and introduced her to other school staff. Even though Cline had participated in a five-year preparation program with a full-year internship, she still benefited from Roberts's gentle guidance.

As a requirement of the Centerville mentoring program, Roberts and Cline observed each other teaching. They also had four days of release time, which they used to visit other schools and gather instructional ideas. During the course of her induction year, Cline frequently sought Roberts's input on her classroom practice. "Barb made me feel real successful, but she also let me fall a few times," Cline admits. "She supported me, yet she gave me the space to try new things and see how they worked."

At one point, Cline experienced classroom management difficulties and sought Roberts's assistance. Together, they devised a new classroom management program, and within three weeks, Cline's class exhibited significant improvement. "Barb also helped me to avoid burning out," Cline says. "When she saw that I was constantly working quite late, she advised me to go home. She told me that I might have flawless bulletin boards, but if I was physically exhausted, I wouldn't be very good for my students."

Making Mentoring Meaningful

Roberts, who serves on the Centerville School District mentoring committee, believes that the success of mentoring new teachers hinges on systemic support of the mentoring program. In Centerville, the union local negotiated release time and $1,000 stipends for mentor teachers. "The stipends and credit hours are a real incentive for our mentors," Roberts says. "They also formalize the program, give it credibility, and communicate that the program is valued." For Cline, Roberts's protégé, the stipend also made a difference. "Knowing she was being paid kept me from feeling I was imposing on her," she says.

Although schools have developed many models of mentoring, successful programs share key components. "Having leaders, particularly principals, who are committed to the notion of helping beginning teachers find success, makes a critical difference," says Rowley, who serves as a university connection with mentor teachers in Centerville.

In addition to tangible incentives and district support, mentors also require specialized professional development. "Educators need to be trained to know how to effectively help new teachers," Roberts says. In Centerville, experienced teachers apply to become mentors and participate in coursework. And each year, the district mentoring committee gives careful consideration to the matches between mentors and new teachers. Mindy Cline believes that she benefited from the careful selection process. "As a reading resource teacher, Barb really understood my content concerns," Cline says. "But because she wasn't a member of my teaching team, I felt comfortable seeking her advice on my team's dynamics."

Feedback and Time

Many mentor-training programs focus on teaching how to provide appropriate feedback to new teachers. "The support providers give descriptions, not value judgments, about what they observe in the new teacher's classroom," Janicki explains. Although mentors may help new teachers learn and understand state standards for teacher practice, the role of the mentors is to be confidential support providers—not formal evaluators. In California, this supportive role is exemplified through the individual induction plans that mentors develop with beginning teachers and that are based on the state's standards for teaching.

For Janicki, time is the fundamental resource for effective teacher support programs. "Doing this well requires a time commitment on the part of schools," he says. "Policymakers need to recognize that support providers need time to work with beginning teachers. Not allowing adequate time can doom a program. You can't do this on the fly."

Professional Payoffs

Although mentoring a new teacher in California costs nearly $5,000 (including administrative expenses), studies show that the approach is financially effective. By reducing the teacher dropout rate, the California New Teacher Project, the precursor to today's state effort, saved money on recruitment and rehiring (California Commission on Teacher Credentialing, 1992).

The budget books tell only part of the story. The greatest benefits of supporting new teachers can be found in the classroom. "I wouldn't be the same teacher today if it weren't for my mentor," says Cline. "Reflection is a large part of my teaching today because Barb modeled the importance of reflecting on my practice." Mentors, too, benefit from their relationships with beginners. "Mindy brought a lot to me in the area of new curriculum," Roberts notes. "We all become better teachers through these relationships." Following Roberts's lead, Cline, now in her seventh year of teaching, recently pursued the training to become a mentor herself—and continue the cycle of support.

References

California Commission on Teacher Credentialing. (1992). *Success for beginning teachers: The California New Teacher Project*. Sacramento: California Department of Education.

Fuller, F. F. (1969). Concerns of teachers: A developmental conceptualization. *American Educational Research Journal*, 6(2), 207–226.

Gonzales, F., & Sosa, A. S. (1993, March). How do we keep teachers in our classrooms? The TNT response. *IDRA Newsletter, 1*, 6–9.

Joan Montgomery Halford is Senior Associate Editor of *Educational Leadership* (e-mail: jhalford@ascd.org).

The Stages of a Teacher's First Year

Ellen Moir

To support new teachers effectively, other educators must understand the phases that novices often experience during their pivotal first year.

First-year teaching is a difficult challenge. Equally challenging is determining how to assist beginning teachers as they enter the profession. Since 1988, the Santa Cruz New Teacher Project, a 16-district consortium led by the University of California, Santa Cruz, has been supporting the efforts of new teachers. After working with nearly 1,500 new teachers, my colleagues and I have noted a number of developmental phases. Although not every new teacher goes through this exact sequence, understanding these phases is useful to educators who support new teachers, including administrators, teacher education faculty, and other support personnel.

New teachers move through several phases: from anticipation, to survival, to disillusionment, to rejuvenation, to reflection, then back to anticipation. Here's a look at the stages, exemplified by excerpts from new teachers' journal entries and end-of-the-year program evaluations.

Anticipation Phase

The anticipation phase begins during the student teaching portion of preservice preparation. The closer that student teachers get to completing their assignment, the more excited and anxious they become about their first teaching position. They tend to romanticize the role of the teacher. New teachers enter classrooms with a tremendous commitment to making a difference and a somewhat idealistic view of how to accomplish their goals. "*I was elated to get the job but terrified about going from the simulated experience of student teaching to being the person completely in charge.*" This feeling of excitement carries new teachers through the first few weeks of school.

Survival Phase

The first month of school is overwhelming for new teachers. They are learning a lot at a rapid pace. Beginning teachers are bombarded with a variety of problems and situations they had not anticipated. Despite teacher education courses and student teaching experience, the realities of teaching on their own catch new teachers off guard. There is so little time and so much to learn. "*I thought I'd be busy—something like student teaching—but this is crazy. I'm constantly running. It's hard to focus on other aspects of my life.*"

During the survival phase, most new teachers struggle to keep their heads above water. They become consumed with the day-to-day routine of teaching. It is not uncommon for new teachers to spend up to 70 hours a week on school work. They have little time to stop and reflect on their experiences.

Particularly overwhelming is the constant need to develop curriculum. Veteran teachers routinely reuse excellent lessons and units from past years. New teachers, still uncertain of what will really work, must develop their lessons for the first time. Even when they depend on textbooks and prepared curriculum, teaching unfamiliar content is enormously time-consuming.

"*I thought there would be more time to get everything done. It's like working three jobs: 7:30–2:30, 2:30–6:00, with more time spent in the evening and on weekends.*" Although tired and surprised by the amount of work, first-year teachers usually maintain a tremendous amount of energy and commitment during the survival phase, and they harbor hope that soon the turmoil will subside.

Disillusionment Phase

After six to eight weeks of nonstop work and stress, new teachers enter the disillusionment phase. The intensity and the length of the phase vary among new teachers. The extensive time commitment, the realization that things are probably not going as smoothly as they would like, and low morale contribute to this period of disenchantment. New teachers begin questioning their commitment and their competence. Many new teachers fall ill during this phase.

Compounding an already difficult situation is the fact that new teachers confront several new events during this time frame: back-to-school night, parent conferences, and their first formal evaluation by the site administrator. Each milestone places an already vulnerable individual in a very stressful situation.

Back-to-school night means giving a speech to parents about plans for the year that are most likely still unclear in the new teacher's mind. Some parents are uneasy when they realize that the teacher is a beginner, and they may pose questions or make demands that intimidate a new teacher.

Parent conferences require new teachers to be highly organized, articulate, tactful, and prepared to confer with parents about each student's progress. This type of communication with parents can be awkward and difficult for beginning teachers. New teachers generally begin with the idea that parents are partners in the learning process, and they are not prepared for parents' concerns or criticisms. These criticisms hit new teachers at a time of waning self-esteem.

Figure 1:
The Phases of a First-Year Teacher's Attitude Toward Teaching

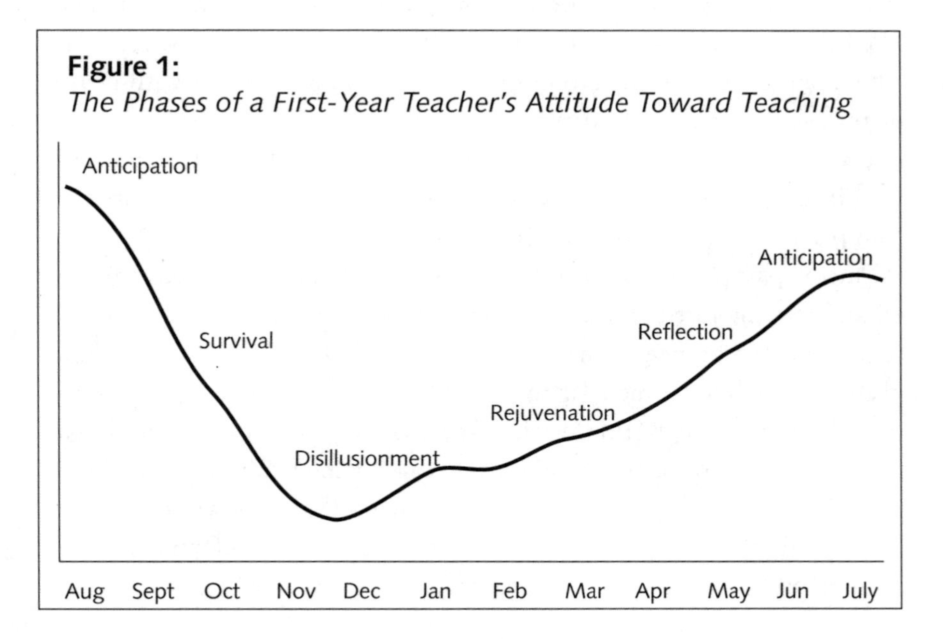

The first formal evaluation by the principal also arrives during the disillusionment phase. Developing and presenting a "showpiece" lesson are time-consuming and stressful. New teachers, uncertain about the evaluation process and anxious about their own competence, question their ability to perform.

During the disillusionment phase, classroom management often becomes a major source of distress. "*I thought I'd be focusing more on curriculum and less on classroom management and discipline. I'm stressed because I have some very problematic students who are low academically, and I think about them every second my eyes are open.*"

At this point, the accumulated stress on new teachers, coupled with months of overwork, provokes complaints from family members and friends. In the disillusionment phase, new teachers express self-doubt, have lower self-esteem, and question their professional commitment. Getting through this phase may be the toughest challenge they face as new teachers.

Rejuvenation Phase

The rejuvenation phase, which generally begins in January, is characterized by a slow improvement in the new teacher's attitude toward teaching. Having a winter break makes a tremendous difference for new teachers. The free time allows them to resume a more normal lifestyle, with plenty of rest, food, exercise, and time for family and friends. The break also offers an opportunity to organize materials and plan curriculum. This breathing space gives new teachers time for reflection and a chance to gain perspective. Most of all, it provides hope.

Putting past problems behind them, new teachers return to school rested and reinvigorated. They now have a better understanding of the system, more acceptance of the realities of teaching, and a sense of accomplishment at having made it through the first, and hardest, part of the school year. Although still months away, the end of school becomes a beacon of hope. By now, new teachers have also gained confidence and better coping skills to prevent or manage problems that they will encounter. During this phase, new teachers focus on curriculum development, long-term planning, and teaching strategies.

"I'm really excited about my story-writing center, although the organization of it has at times been haphazard. Story-writing has definitely revived my journals." The rejuvenation phase tends to last into spring, with many ups and downs along the way. Toward the end of this phase, new teachers begin to voice concerns about whether they can accomplish everything by the end of the school year. They also wonder how their students will perform on tests, once again questioning their own effectiveness as teachers. *"I'm fearful of these big tests. Can you be fired if your kids do poorly? I don't know enough about them to know what I haven't taught, and I'm sure it's a lot."*

Reflection Phase

The reflection phase begins during the last six weeks of school. These final weeks are a particularly invigorating time for first-year teachers. Reflecting back over the year, new teachers highlight events that were successful and those that were not. They think about the various changes that they plan to make the following year in management, curriculum, and teaching strategies. The end is in sight, and they have almost made it; but more important, a vision emerges about what their second year will look like, which brings them to a new phase of anticipation. *"I think that next year I'd like to start the letter puppets earlier to introduce the kids to more letters."*

It is essential that we assist new teachers and ease the transition from student teacher to full-time professional. Recognizing the phases that new teachers go through gives us a framework within which we can begin to design support programs to make the first year of teaching a more positive experience for our new colleagues.

Ellen Moir is Director of the New Teacher Center at the University of California, Santa Cruz, 809 Bay Ave., Capitola, CA 95010.

PART II

CREATING AN INDUCTION PROGRAM

Induction: The First Five Days

Sandra Martin and Kathryn Robbins

A mandatory, structured induction program introduces new teachers to the culture, expectations, and vision of their district and school. The authors describe a five-day introductory structure that kicks off the school year.

You've landed the job. New keys are placed in your hand along with a stack of textbooks. You make your way to Room 207 at the end of the corridor. School begins in two days. You think, now what? What will I do on the first day of class? What will I wear? What will the kids think of me? Will I be too tough? Too nice? When will I find time to read all these materials from the district office?

New teachers often experience this scenario. Overwhelmed with material given out at a district meeting just days before the start of school, teachers don't know what to do first. Read the policy manuals? Start preparing lessons? Develop classroom rules? Most new-teacher induction programs are classic cases of "too little, too late."

The new-teacher induction program at Leyden High Schools in Franklin Park, Illinois, developed out of our need to retain strong teachers. We watched teachers, overwhelmed by the paperwork and responsibilities, struggle to meet the demands of teaching classes, working with parents, and sponsoring cocurricular activities. Some of our most promising teachers chose to leave the profession, or we made the choice to release others at the end of their first year. We had spent a great deal of energy hiring teachers who we thought were good matches for our students and had the potential to be excellent career teachers. We were disappointed as teachers dropped out of the profession.

Our inspiration for change came from Harry Wong, whose work focuses on the importance of strong induction programs not only for new teachers, but also for all teachers new to a district. Wong's work was a catalyst that renewed our energy to change our induction program into one that would truly help teachers be effective from the first day of school forward. Our program incorporates Wong's philosophy and materials.[1]

The Induction Program

Leyden High Schools' new-teacher induction program, entitled "Everything You Ever Wanted to Know About Teaching But Were Afraid to Ask," started in 1996. Approximately 20 to 25 teachers new to the district participate each year. New teachers are notified when hired that enrollment in the class is a condition of tenure. Although teachers are not paid a stipend, they do receive credit toward movement on the salary schedule.

The 30-hour course meets Monday through Friday, 8 a.m until 2 p.m., during the first week of August. We selected early August to give teachers time before the start of school to assimilate new knowledge and to incorporate new ideas into their lesson planning. The course combines an overview of effective teaching principles and practices with an orientation to the district, the building, the department, the staff, the students, and the community.

Although our school district employs approximately 210 teachers to serve more than 3,000 students in two public high schools in the suburban Chicago area, this program could be easily modified to meet the needs of smaller or larger districts. Because the teachers do not receive monetary compensation and the trainers are full-time administrators, costs for this home-grown program are less than $100 for each teacher.

Participants in this program can expect to

- Become acquainted with the district's culture, expectations, and vision;
- Understand the expectations of the superintendent, the board of education, the administration, and the students;
- Be armed with the knowledge to be successful;
- Feel more confident and comfortable with their supervisors, one another, and the infrastructure of the school; and

- Know all the things that we wish we had known before we started teaching.

The Program Structure

Each day of the five-day program has a theme to lend structure. Content is grouped around each theme in order of relevance to the new teacher. Administrators in the district, each leading his or her own area of specialization, conduct the class sessions. This practice lends some variety to the presentations and illustrates that members of the administration work as a team and that all are committed to the success of the new teachers. Faculty members run specialized sessions, for example, on technology.

We designed our program to model effective lesson design, classroom procedures, positive attitudes, high expectations, effective use of daily homework, and effective use of time to maximize learning. We want teachers not only to be told "how things should be," but also to experience how it *feels* to be part of a well-run classroom.

Day One: *Culture, Expectations, and Vision*

New teachers are introduced to administrators and key people in the district, learn the district philosophy and mission, glean a better understanding of the hierarchy of the system, and develop a perception of the expectations for all teachers in the district.

Teachers tour each building and ride a school bus to tour the district. They learn about student and community demographics and receive bell schedules, their own schedules, class lists, supervisory assignments, and room keys. We explain these aspects of teaching in detail, and everyone has an opportunity to ask questions and discuss information.

Day Two: *Positive Expectations*

We believe that teachers' positive expectations are crucial for student success. New teachers engage in a variety of learning activities to foster this understanding as well as to learn the importance of the first day of school, how to select role models, how to encourage appropriate student-teacher relationships, and how to cultivate successful parent-teacher relationships. For example, teachers write about their ideal classroom, then share their vision with their classmates. The conversations lead to common themes, attitudes, and classroom climate. Next, the teachers discuss instructional practice that fosters their ideal classroom.

Day Three: *Classroom Management*

Classroom management, or the lack of it, often makes or breaks a beginning teacher. Workshop time is spent role playing, practicing appropriate interventions, writing supporting documents, and reviewing the resources and interventions available to the faculty. In addition, teachers learn about attendance procedures and sanctions for students. Individual classroom management plans are discussed and developed, structured around rules, consequences, and rewards.

The class generates and shares responses to the "Seven Things Kids Want to Know on the First Day of School."

- Am I in the right room?
- Where am I supposed to sit?
- What are the rules in this classroom?
- What will I be doing this year?
- How will I be graded?
- Who is the teacher as a person?
- Will the teacher treat me like a human being?

New teachers also spend time developing a repertoire of procedures for routine tasks, such as getting students' attention, collecting papers, and dealing with absent students. Our technology director conducts hands-on training on using a computer grade book. The teachers learn about all the technology that the district offers teachers and students.

Day Four: *Mastery and Cooperative Learning*

In true graduate school style, participants teach one another about instructional design to ensure content mastery by developing effective lessons that use cooperative learning and designing appropriate assessment tools. New teachers also learn about the district's instructional goals and the curriculum development process.

We also review the district's evaluation system. Teachers learn what to expect in terms of who will visit their classroom, when observations will take place, and what criteria will be used for their assessment. We end the discussion by explaining the part that evaluation plays in their continued employment in the district. Teachers also learn that professional attire is an expectation of the district and will influence students' perceptions of them. All of this sets the stage for the formal evaluation process. We also let teachers know about the professional development options available to them.

Day Five: *Professionalism and Expectations*

The morning begins with a "tour" of a demonstration classroom. Successful veteran teachers who have participated in the induction program and have implemented many of the procedures and routines learned in the program demonstrate them for the new group of teachers. We visit the demonstration classroom where the veteran gives the tour and explains the organization of the room and its effects on classroom climate and student learning.

Next, a panel of our top-notch teachers offers insight into working in our district and enjoying the teaching profession. They respond to the following questions:

- What did you learn your first year of teaching?
- What would you have done differently?
- What gives you joy in teaching?
- What keeps you going?

Each year we are amazed that such simple questions evoke such strong emotion and inspiration. Often participants and viewers are moved to tears.

The day ends with certificates and a graduation ceremony that has become a pep rally. Teachers cheer one another as they come forward to accept their framed certificate. We encourage our teachers to display the award along with their diplomas in their classroom.

An important part of our staff development is the care and feeding of our teachers. Each day, a different restaurant caters breakfast and lunch.

The meals are the vehicle for increased interaction among the teachers and the administrators, who come to lunch each day to mingle with the new teachers. We also give the new teachers small gifts each day: colored chalk, grading pens, software, Leyden High Schools folders, and school booster items. This attention to detail illustrates our commitment to our "you are special and we're glad you're here" philosophy.

Program Evaluation

We ask participants to evaluate the course at the end of the program. This anonymous form gives us feedback for improving our class for our next group of recruits. The teachers' reactions have been positive:

From experienced teachers

> I realized that teaching is not a random art. There are identifiable things that effective teachers do, and I can do them also.

> The best in-service class I've been to in 20 years.

From first-year teachers

> Speaking of positive role models! You two were not only obvious examples of professionalism, but were models of organization, preparation, high energy, intentional, invitational teaching; and creativity. You really practiced what you preached. Thank you.

> I'll remember the effort all of the people made to welcome us and to help us feel better prepared.

> I thought I was prepared, but after this class, I wonder where I'd be right now without it.

Continuing Education

This program doesn't end after the first week in August. The last activity for the new-teacher induction program asks teachers to complete a final assignment prior to the first day of school. They submit one lesson, based on either cooperative or mastery learning, that they will use during the first three weeks of school and that incorporates the elements of lesson design discussed in our class.

Several days before the start of school, new teachers attend a formal dinner with the board of education. The board president explains the district's philosophy of good schools and good teaching and stresses the importance of valuing the abilities of our students and preparing for class each day. The next day begins with an overview of insurance benefits, payroll procedures, and other necessary housekeeping details. Next, new teachers participate in round-table discussions with groups of students, parents, second-year teachers, veteran teachers, and guidance counselors. Finally, they have lunch with their assigned department mentors and department chairs.

Once school begins, the new teachers meet monthly with their building principals and as often as needed with their mentors. We also host one or two class reunions during the year so that we can bring together the new teachers to gain additional feedback about our induction program and to renew friendships.

Because Illinois has changed the duration of probationary teaching to four years, we are planning to add several courses that will contribute to teachers' knowledge and skills during years two, three, and four. All these courses will be part of our internal summer and after-school staff development program, called "Leyden University," which features 15- and 30-hour courses on such topics as Spanish for Educators, Creating Your Own Web Site, and Cooperative Learning. The school awards successful completion with movement on the salary schedule.

All in all, these efforts have paid off for the district. Our retention rate for new teachers ranges from 85 to 95 percent. Perhaps more important is the response from supervisors: "These new teachers don't look like new teachers." The induction program increases confidence and skills and, ultimately, improves the success of our students.

Note

[1]Wong, H., & Wong, R. (1998). *The first days of school.* Sunnyvale, CA: Harry K. Wong Publications.

Sandra Martin is Assistant Superintendent for Homewood-Flossmoor High School, 999 Kedzie Ave., Flossmoor, IL 60422 (e-mail: SMartin@Kiwi.dep.anl.gov). **Kathryn Robbins** is Superintendent for Leyden High Schools, 3400 N. Rose St., Franklin Park, IL 60131.

First Things First: How to Set Up An Induction Program

Annette Breaux

A school district in Thibodaux, Louisiana, implemented a successful induction program to help ease the transition for its new teachers. The author outlines the steps needed for planning and implementation.

By now, many educators know what induction is: a structured training process for new teachers. They know that research supports the benefits of induction and that districts offering induction programs are increasing teacher effectiveness and retaining more qualified teachers. They know that after going through an induction process, new teachers feel more confident about their teaching. What many educators do not know, however, is *how* to go about setting up an induction program for their new teachers. Four years ago, we in Lafourche Parish Schools, Thibodaux, Louisiana, found ourselves in that situation.

How We Got Started

At the recommendation of Harry Wong, we contacted five school districts already implementing successful induction programs. All these districts were eager to share information on their programs and suggestions for developing our own program. Instead of reinventing the wheel, we decided to combine the best of the best. We found out what the most successful districts around the country were doing and built on that information.

Within six months, we launched our Framework for Inducting, Retaining, and Supporting Teachers (FIRST) new-teacher induction program. Now completing our third year of inducting more than 200 new teachers, we are proud to say that 99 percent of our certified new teachers remain in teaching and that 88 percent are still teaching in our school district. Superintendent Malcolm Duplantis says, "Our new-teacher induction program has increased teacher competence and confidence throughout our school system. It is, without a doubt, the best thing we have ever done for our new teachers." Supervisor of Personnel Elmo Broussard adds, "Retaining qualified teachers is a problem that has always plagued us. Induction may be our solution."

The FIRST Year

The induction process begins with four highly structured days in early August, during which first-year teachers learn the rudiments of classroom management, instructional strategies, discipline, first-day classroom procedures, district policies and procedures, and lesson planning. Each participant receives a copy of *The First Days of School* (Wong & Wong, 1998), along with a new-teacher binder. The binder contains a letter of welcome from the superintendent; a copy of the district's philosophy; checklists to aid in teaching preparation; tips for new teachers; and sections for faculty and staff lists, school policies and procedures, class rosters and schedules, classroom management plans, bell and duty schedules, and student information. The superintendent, assistant superintendent, curriculum coordinators, and curriculum supervisors welcome new teachers. And the induction process officially begins.

The new teachers then become "students," and the three curriculum coordinators become their teachers. We model what we want them to do with their students in their classrooms. Because the curriculum coordinators are former classroom teachers, our advice stems from experience. We enjoy sharing our most successful accomplishments, our most embarrassing moments, and our most heartwarming experiences in the classroom. Because we will continue to work closely with the new teachers during their first few years of teaching, we know that it is imperative to establish a trusting, supportive relationship with them. The induction process provides a framework for such a relationship.

The four days are highly structured, and the pace is steady. The classroom is work oriented, and the inductees are actively involved in their learning. Day one focuses on classroom management. To model the importance of procedures and routines in the classroom, we establish actual procedures and routines for our induction classroom. Days two and three address the first days of school, instructional strategies, assessment techniques, positive discipline techniques, and strategies to meet individual student differences and to work with parents. Though we cover a variety of topics during the four days, the primary focus is classroom management (see Tips for Classroom Management, below).

On day three, a second-year teacher talks to the new teachers about the value of the induction process. This teacher entertains questions from the inductees and shares personal first-year experiences.

On the fourth day, a darkened room is aglow with candles, and soft music echoes as participants stand in a circle, holding hands and listening to a poem entitled "I Am a Teacher" (Canfield & Hansen, 1993). There is rarely a dry eye in the room as each inductee comes forward to receive a certificate of achievement along with hugs and well wishes from their teachers. This is followed by a luncheon at which new teachers meet mentor teachers, principals, school board members, and administrative staff members. On the afternoon of the fourth day, the new teachers visit demonstration classrooms specific to their grade levels and receive advice and instruction from our most successful veteran teachers. For the initial four days of induction, participants are paid stipends.

Tips for Classroom Management

- Maintain an organized, pleasant, functional classroom environment.
- Always greet your students at the door.
- Never arrive unprepared.
- Adopt only a few rules, and establish procedures for all activities.
- Give copies of your rules and procedures to students and parents.
- Engage learners in meaningful activities.
- Maximize instructional time.
- Enable all students to experience success.
- Nip potential problems by being proactive.
- Treat all students with dignity.

The induction process does not end there. A curriculum coordinator observes each new teacher several times throughout the year. These strictly informal observations are tools for offering ongoing encouragement, support, and assistance to the new teachers. New teachers are also required to participate in the Louisiana Teacher Assistance and Assessment Program, with formal observations determining certification decisions. All teachers participating in this program receive two additional days of training on the Louisiana Components of Effective Teaching. Although the induction process is in no way tied to the state assessment program, effective teaching is the focus of both.

In April, inductees return for a one-day New Teacher Induction Review. On this day, new teachers address ongoing concerns, share first-year teaching experiences, and receive additional instruction.

Year Two

During the second year of the induction process, the curriculum coordinators continue to work closely with the new teachers. Classroom observations are ongoing. In addition, second-year teachers attend four half-day sessions to receive further training in classroom management, instructional strategies, authentic assessment, and instructional decision making. During one segment of each session, participants pose questions, voice concerns, seek solutions to common classroom problems, and share personal classroom experiences. Again, participants are paid stipends. At this time, we are adding a third year to the program.

Mentoring the New Teacher

Just as the terms *classroom management* and *discipline* are often mistaken for synonyms, so are the terms *mentoring* and *induction*. Though discipline is an integral component of classroom management, it remains just that—one important part. Likewise, mentoring is only one component of induction, albeit a vital one.

As part of the state assessment program, each new teacher is assigned a mentor for one year. These mentors receive three days of intensive training along with ongoing staff development and support from the curriculum coordinators. The mentors provide each new teacher a built-in, on-site support system. When asked how she felt about having a mentor, one new middle school teacher replied, "My mentor teacher saved my life! Because of her, I made it through my first year of teaching."

The Role of the Principal

After the new teachers attend the initial four days of induction training in early August, they are not yet officially inducted. They have only begun what will become a three-year induction process.

To ensure consistency between what is promoted during the initial training and what will be promoted in the schools, principals receive awareness training before the actual induction process begins. Within their schools, the principals take over by providing support, guidance, and encouragement to the new teachers, along with opportunities for ongoing assistance and staff development.

Noelee Brooks, principal of Sixth Ward Middle School in Thibodaux, Louisiana, participates in the initial four days of induction by providing some of the actual training. New teachers hear—from a principal's viewpoint—what will be expected of them regarding dress, attitudes, and general professionalism. Brooks also offers words of encouragement and advice for new teachers regarding first-day procedures.

A Worthwhile Investment

According to the National Commission on Teaching and America's Future (1996),

> On the whole, the school reform movement has ignored the obvious. What teachers know and can do makes the crucial difference in what children learn. And the ways school systems organize their work makes a big difference in what teachers can accomplish. New courses, tests, and curriculum reforms can be important starting points, but they are meaningless if teachers cannot use them well. Policies can only improve schools if the people in them are armed with the knowledge, skills, and supports they need. Student learning in this country will improve only when we focus our efforts on improving teaching (p. 5).

Just four short years ago, we had a vision. Our goal was to implement an induction program that would ease the way for new teachers by providing ongoing training and support. The results? Overwhelming enthusiasm from new teachers, mentors, administrators, school board members, and the community, and increased retention of more confident, competent, qualified new teachers who influence the lives of thousands of students. We managed all this within a budget of $50,000 a year. This is a small price to pay for an investment on which no dollar amount can possibly be placed—our children, our future.

References

Canfield, J., & Hansen, M. V. (1993). *Chicken soup for the soul.* Deerfield Beach, FL: Health Communication.

National Commission on Teaching and America's Future. (1996). *What matters most: Teaching for America's future*. New York: Author.

Wong, H., & Wong, R. (1998). *The first days of school.* Sunnyvale, CA: Harry K. Wong Publications.

Annette Breaux is Curriculum Coordinator for Lafourche Parish School Board, 110 Bowie Rd., Thibodaux, LA 70301 (e-mail: abreaux.pac@lafourche.k12.la.us).

The Elements of a Supportive Induction Program

Aileen Heidkamp with Janet Shapiro

How do we make novice teachers feel welcome, connected, and listened to in their new school? The authors provide tips for those who want to build their own strong induction program.

My first year teaching was like . . .

- a psychological battery test. All my strengths and weaknesses were revealed and put on display for the students.
- deep-sea diving in Hawaii. It's been beautiful and exciting, with some "rough" objects underfoot.
- being on a treadmill for which I was not in shape. The pace was too quick for me!
- trying to hold up a 10-ton weight. The school obviously has many procedures and contingency plans. Keeping up with and learning these systems requires much time and effort.
- a wild roller-coaster ride that hasn't slowed down yet. Though it's been fun and exciting, I am looking forward to eventually stopping. I must admit, though, I like the ride a lot!

—First- and second-year teachers at
Sacred Heart Cathedral Preparatory School

Like many schools, Sacred Heart Cathedral Preparatory makes concentrated efforts to welcome new students. We sponsor freshmen orientation, in which older students show younger students the ropes. We invite freshmen and their families to a freshmen family picnic. We give new students tours of the school, show them where to buy books, and demonstrate how to open their lockers. But if we warmly welcome our freshmen—who will spend four years at school—shouldn't we do as much, if not more, to welcome, orient, and support new teachers?

Effective Support

Long-time teachers know that learning to teach is a process. Dynamic, energetic teachers continually experiment with new ideas and methodology. They renew and review their practices. Devoted teachers, those who exert positive influence and change, constitute a school's most valuable resource. How does a school attract, train, and retain those individuals who are or can become such teachers? Certainly, this does not happen easily.

Teaching is an unusual profession because the first-year teacher in most cases is assigned to the same tasks in and out of the classroom as a long-time veteran. In some cases, the novice teacher performs just as well, but administrators and veterans must invest significant time and resources to foster a new teacher's development into a dynamic educator. This investment helps faculty develop a positive, professional attitude, which ultimately creates a better learning environment for students.

A new-teacher support program should be designed to meet the specific needs of a particular school. What is unique about working in your particular environment, and what should a new person know to succeed? Answers to these questions can form the basis of an effective support program.

In our case, Sacred Heart Cathedral Preparatory is a coeducational, Catholic secondary school in urban San Francisco. More than 1,200 students attend the school, which employs approximately 90 teachers. Over the last eight years, the faculty has grown significantly. When we began to orient new teachers as a group in 1991–92, we simply welcomed them with a special lunch before the first day of school, gave them a tour of the facility, and spoke to them about the school's history. Then we hoped that their teacher training would prove enough. Now, these activities form the mere basis of a much more developed program. Each year, we learn a bit more about the scope of new teachers' needs within our school; in response, we have gradually formulated our current new-teacher support program.

The following tips, which are based on our experience, can help administrators and veteran teachers create new-teacher programs that anticipate needs and support new teachers in those first crucial years.

Step One: Provide Administrative Support and Direction

Our experience tells us that to succeed, new teachers need to know where to turn for help.

- As early as possible in the school year, identify key individuals to new teachers and explain the kind of positive support these individuals will offer.
- Schedule one-on-one meetings with the administrator or faculty member whose responsibility it is to foster, monitor, and celebrate the novice teacher's successes.

Our director of professional development has a primary responsibility to support and guide new teachers. (Please note: We consider *all* teachers new to our school *new teachers*, even those who may have taught in other schools.) The director of professional development coordinates the new-teacher support program and provides individual assistance to new teachers. She acts as the resource, advisor, and guide. In the first weeks of school, she makes frequent contacts with new teachers. She is also part of the formal observation and evaluation process; her frequent observations of classes early in the school year help teachers avoid potential pitfalls and reaffirm their positive efforts. She guides teachers' self-evaluations and helps them in setting attainable goals.

The director of professional development also works with department chair to ensure that new teachers receive the necessary curriculum direction and support. These two individuals also assist a new teacher in identifying other resources within departments. Though our school does not have a formal mentoring program, most novice teachers find a veteran to fulfill this role.

Step Two: Welcome New Teachers

Teachers generally meet their new challenges with a mixture of excitement and apprehension. Early in the school year, administrators and veteran faculty members need to share their enthusiasm and allay their fears. Simple efforts make significant differences.

- Make sure you formally welcome new teachers. Let them know you are happy to have them.

- Invite them into your community by clearly identifying who is who and who does what.
- Make them feel at home. If possible, invite them to share a meal with administrators, department chairs, and prospective mentors.
- Don't forget to identify people to whom they should direct questions, however small.

We meet with teachers over the course of three days before the start of the school year. These meetings have various goals. First, we encourage them to get to know one another; in many cases, they will be one another's emotional lifelines. We introduce key administrators, who address the group with brief, pertinent information. New teachers also receive a tour of our facilities. As early as possible, we give them keys to their classrooms and schedule time for them to get settled. Brief sessions introduce them to the main facets of the school—its history, philosophy, student activities, and athletics.

Though it sounds like a lot of information to digest, we make every attempt to avoid overwhelming new teachers. This orientation includes a simple lunch with department chairs, administrators, and second-year teachers, who share helpful pointers on getting through the first year. A more formal dinner with the two religious communities who administer the school also occurs during the week.

Step Three: Maintain Frequent Contact

As the school year begins, new teachers need forums in which they can ask questions and receive vital information.

- Provide a designated administrator or department chair to meet with teachers on a regular basis.
- Give new teachers immediate feedback on classroom observations early in the school year.

During the first week of school, our director of professional development holds two meetings to ensure that new teachers feel comfortable and to field questions or problems. During the second through sixth weeks of school, we conduct weekly "business" meetings with the group of new teachers; subsequently, meetings occur at least once a month. Discussion items cover a wide range of information: roles and responsibilities at upcoming events, attendance procedures, the school calendar and daily schedule, the school computer system, situations with students, and procedures to obtain necessary supplies.

In addition, the director of professional development and department chairs make informal classroom observations. New teachers need immediate feedback. In our experience, most feedback affirms their enthusiastic efforts. And by identifying areas of difficulty as early as possible, we give novice teachers immediate opportunities to make positive changes.

Step Four: Allow Time for Professional Development and Professional Relationships

New teachers need to understand the school's culture and to build professional relationships.

- Create opportunities for new teachers to discuss professional issues with veterans and administrators. Do not assume that conversations about methodology, procedures, and school culture and traditions will automatically take place informally.
- Support all teachers in their efforts to develop and pursue a plan of professional development. Encourage groups with common interests to participate together.

We hold monthly seminars in which new teachers discuss various issues with veteran faculty members and administrators. Topics include classroom environments, assessment, professional roles and relationships, the school's technological resources, and personal health maintenance. In these seminars, teachers discuss their experiences, concerns, and questions in small groups. Panelists also make presentations followed by questions and answers. New teachers hear veterans' stories with interest and learn from them, especially when teachers share experiences about their own growth as educators. These forums also encourage new teachers to ask questions and to discover new resources in their colleagues.

This year, our new-teacher support program will expand again. We believe that the support that we offer new teachers needs to continue after their first year. Therefore, we are developing a more comprehensive in-house professional development program. We will sponsor in-service training, in which topics will change each year. This first year, we plan to focus on brain-based learning. The entire faculty will attend the session; as this aspect of the program develops, teachers new to our school will be able to witness our faculty's commitment to evolving as teachers and learners.

Step Five: Conduct a Self-Evaluation

The most direct way of knowing whether you are giving new teachers what they need is to ask them. After every monthly seminar, we ask teachers about the value and effectiveness of the discussion. During meetings with groups and individuals, the director of professional development asks teachers what help they need and solicits their questions. We make refinements and adjustments on the basis of their responses.

We think that the best way to know if teachers feel supported is to evaluate whether they are comfortable enough to ask questions. When new teachers pose questions, even small ones, they demonstrate their trust. Educators know that questions form the basis of a learning process. By showing that we are open and responsive to them, we will encourage new teachers to grow into dynamic members of our educational community.

And finally, new teachers can support and learn from one another. The following advice from our new teachers to other novice teachers also helps us know what new teachers need to succeed:

- Be sure to set aside time for yourself, completely away from school and work.
- If you have a concern, don't hold back. Be sure to ask someone for advice.
- Don't do too many other things, such as taking classes, during your first year.
- Get interested in the students. Go to their games and plays.
- Be confident and have faith. Focus on the nobility of what you endeavor.

- Plan, plan ahead.
- Keep breathing.

Aileen Heidkamp is the English Department Chair and **Janet Shapiro** is the Director of Professional Development at Sacred Heart Cathedral Preparatory, 1055 Ellis St., San Francisco, CA 94109 (e-mail: aileheid@shcp.edu).

Creating Conditions for Teacher Success

Barb Knudsen and Sue Zapf

This new-teacher induction-mentoring program builds bonds among participants while it strengthens their professional competence.

On the day before the fall workshop begins, Justin, a first-year teacher, feels anxious. Although he knows the location of the high school, the name of the principal, and the classes he will be teaching, he knows little else. He believes that after three days of workshops, he will be ready for the first day of school. However, early in the workshop, he becomes overwhelmed as he discovers that all but two hours are filled with district meetings, faculty meetings, department meetings, and new-teacher meetings.

As his mentor leaves on the third day, she notices a worried Justin staring at his vacant room. Thinking that she needs to give him some support, she says, "Always feel free to stop by with any questions you have." Justin has only one: "How am I supposed to be ready for students on Monday?" Sound typical? Unfortunately, this scenario is repeated annually in school districts throughout the country.

Lakeville Senior High, a rapidly growing school in a Minneapolis-St. Paul suburb, hires an average of 10 new teachers each year to accommodate a 10 percent growth in student population. As members of the staff, we were disappointed with the retention rate of our first-year teachers. Although we had a mentor program, some of our new teachers were unhappy, isolated, and ineffective. As a result, some did not return for a second year. The practice of merely assigning a mentor to each new faculty member was not working. Its intention was good; its effect was mediocre.

Knowing that teachers create conditions for student success in their classrooms, we rethought our mentoring process by directing that same belief toward teachers and schools. To create conditions for new-teacher success, we designed a mentoring process that prepares teachers socially, emotionally, and academically for the school year. Lisa White, a new teacher at LHS, describes the process as "a trademark of an invested school district. Not only is it an investment of resources and staff, but it is also an obvious investment in students."

A Redesigned Program

The mentoring process begins in the summer with a series of five voluntary meetings. After an initial meeting that includes a building tour and a getting-acquainted session, subsequent meetings focus on teacher professionalism, school policies and procedures, classroom management, school technology, state graduation standards, and instructional strategies and evaluation. By conducting these meetings over two months, we create an inviting environment that helps new staff members develop relationships among themselves, prepares them for the upcoming school year, and teaches them the responsibilities of a classroom teacher. During this time, new teachers meet their mentors, each of whom works with three or four new staff members. The mentors volunteer their time, energy, and expertise to any teacher new to our school. Two mentor coordinators, a teacher and an administrator, initiate the process. "The summer sessions," new teacher Ted Schmidt states,

> helped me build camaraderie with my fellow new staff members, acclimated me to the building and its myriad resources, acquainted me with school policies, offered me practical advice regarding classroom management, and helped me prepare for the first day of school.

Program Results

When we began this process, we were not confident what aspects of the program would be the most beneficial. After two years, however, several areas have become significant. First, the time spent getting to know one another on the first evening becomes the foundation of the program's success. During that evening, we ask each staff member to draw a personal map explaining how he or she arrived at Lakeville High School. After we model our own journeys, we send the meeting participants to the cafeteria for about 15 minutes with large sheets of papers and markers to draw their maps. When they return, they take as long as they need to tell their stories. These drawings highlight their personal and professional journeys before they arrived at Lakeville Senior High. Although some maps are limited to family and college experiences, others include travels, previous careers, personal philosophies, and humorous anecdotes. We smile at one another's successes and sigh at one another's heartbreaks.

On this night, relationships emerge; by summer's end, they have developed into friendships. Shannon Bry, a new staff member, comments, "By the end of the summer sessions, we bonded as both educators and friends."

Another significant component of the summer session is the discussion about classroom management. Our school expects teachers to hand out their classroom policies to students within the first few days of school. The summer sessions allow new staff to think through and discuss various policies before actually developing and implementing their own. Although classroom management is the highest concern for first-year teachers, everyone expresses a need to learn the school's spoken and unspoken cultures, specific policies, and teacher-evaluation procedures.

In the final summer session, new staff become familiar with the evaluation, or performance review, process. Not only are they introduced to the specific procedures and forms, but also they are told of its underlying purpose: to help teachers become better teachers. As a result, new staff feel less intimidated and more welcomed by the process.

Once the school year begins, new teachers have two meetings a month—one large-group meeting with the mentor coordinator and one small-group meeting with their mentor and the others in their group. The intent of the large-group meetings is to continue teacher training. The first meeting of the year answers the question, What didn't we tell you? Other meetings focus on specific topics, including parent-teacher conferences, special-services information, more classroom management techniques, instructional strategies from which all students can benefit, and time management. In contrast, the purpose of the small-group meetings is to respond directly to teacher-generated questions and concerns.

The underlying benefit of having large- and small-group meetings is the increase in collegial relationships among the teachers, which promote an inviting environment for sharing what is on their minds. Ted Schmidt comments,

> Both the small- and large-group sessions during the year help me maintain my camaraderie with my fellow teachers and expose me to and provide me with effective methods of dealing with issues and situations that either I may not have encountered yet or about which I have questions and concerns.

Harry McLenighan, Lakeville High School's principal, has observed the development and implementation of the mentorship process over the past two years.

> An effective new-teacher mentoring program is an important component of every school's staff development effort. However, at Lakeville Senior High, where we grow by 150 students and 10 teachers every year, it's absolutely essential. Fortunately, ours is an exceptionally effective program. I measure the program's success in two ways: my observations of new staff and new staff's comments about the program. Both measures confirm my enthusiastic assessment of the LHS Mentor Program. In the past two years, we have had just 1 teacher out of 25 whom we have not retained. That's a significant improvement in the retention rate.

Mentors have also expressed enthusiasm for the mentoring process. Ken Williams, a mentor to four teachers during the 1998–99 school year, stated,

> I have really enjoyed this experience. It's great to work with teachers who are from a variety of departments. Also, it provides a great vehicle for assisting new teachers, offering them one-on-one interaction and small-group intimacy that the larger group doesn't always allow. I found that I had a chance to look at my own methods and commitments in this role.

As educators, we must believe that schools and districts can create the conditions for teacher success. We must do it through a mentorship process that Susan Link, a 1997–98 new staff member, describes as one that "sets new people up for success in an unfamiliar environment."

We must make new teachers feel welcome; we must make them feel valuable; most important, we must make them feel that we want them to be successful. If we do, Justin and other new staff can spend their first year, as Heather Sullivan, a new teacher last year, describes, "focusing our attention on teaching instead of on surviving."

Barb Knudsen is Director of Curriculum and Instruction for Lakeville, Minnesota, School District #194 (e-mail: bwknudsen@isd194.k12.mn.us). **Sue Zapf** is a communications teacher at Lakeville Senior High School, 19600 Ipava Ave., Lakeville, MN 55044 (e-mail: sczapf@isd194.k12.mn.us).

PART III

MAKING MENTORING MEANINGFUL

Mentors Matter

Mary Brooks

The Beginning Teacher Mentor Program in Iowa demonstrates that mentors who collaborate with beginning teachers produce win-win situations within the whole school.

As we know from the titles of many recent publications, mentoring has become a hot topic. Mentors are becoming a career essential because the benefits of mentoring are so tangible. To create a more supportive and successful environment for educators, we created one effective form of mentoring—our Beginning Teacher Mentor Program in the West Des Moines, Iowa, schools.

The Beginning Teacher Mentor Program

Our district serves more than 50,000 people who live in the western portion of Polk County, Iowa. Covering 36.6 square miles, the district has grown up around a former railroad center, Valley Junction, and the farmland north and south of the Raccoon River. We are next door to the state capital, Des Moines.

In 1996, I became site coordinator for the Beginning Teacher Mentor Program—a position that grew out of a two-year pilot project that I wrote a grant for and implemented at Indian Hills Junior High. Funded as a teacher mentor through staff development in 1994–96, I had release time to research mentoring programs and mentor first- and second-year teachers in my building. Currently, I serve half-time as the site coordinator for the district Beginning Teacher Mentor Program; in the other half, I teach three junior high language arts classes.

Every first-year teacher in our school district is assigned a master teacher mentor by the building principal. Mentors work with their assigned new teachers for two years (for a job description, see Figure 1). Eighteen first-year mentors, 14 first-year teachers, and 14 second-year mentors and second-year teachers are involved in the program. Also, a number of new to the district but experienced special teachers—art, physical education, Extended Learning Program, ESL, foreign language, and music—work with curriculum mentors. For the most part, first-year mentors are site- and curriculum-based and receive a $250 stipend. Second-year mentors receive $200.

Figure 1

Job Description of a Mentor Teacher

JOB TITLE: Beginning Mentor Teacher

CLASSIFICATION: Teacher

IMMEDIATE SUPERVISOR: District Site Coordinator, Beginning-Mentor Teacher Program

I. JOB SUMMARY

Provide expertise and ongoing support and professional growth opportunities to enhance the skills and effectiveness of beginning teachers.

II. QUALIFICATIONS

- A. Abilities
  1. Ability to model effective teaching strategies
  2. Ability to work in a collaborative manner
  3. Ability to maintain confidentiality
  4. Ability to manage time effectively
- B. Knowledge
  1. Knowledge of research-based effective teaching strategies
  2. Knowledge of instructional effectiveness
- C. Demonstrated Skills
  1. Professional competence
  2. Effective verbal and nonverbal communication
  3. Interpersonal skills of caring, kindness, and understanding
- D. Experience
  1. Subject-area or grade-level experience
  2. Three or more years of successful teaching experience

III. RESPONSIBILITIES

- A. Attend training as required
- B. Provide expertise and ongoing support
- C. Visit new teacher's classroom and provide feedback

In August, before school starts, first-year mentors receive a half-day of training and spend a half-day with their new teacher. During the school year, first-year mentors attend four New Teacher Support Group meetings for additional training. Second-year mentors meet as a large group once during the second semester. During their training, mentors discuss such topics as the role of a mentor; the needs, problems, and phases of beginning teachers; observation and feedback strategies; and effective teaching strategies. Our classroom observation system also emphasizes effective teaching practices. Through this process, our school district embraces teacher education as a goal, just as we embrace the education of children as a goal.

A Win-Win Combination

In *The Seven Habits of Highly Effective People*, author Stephen Covey labels Habit 4 "Think Win-Win."[1] Our Beginning Teacher Mentor Program produces a win-win situation for everyone involved by seeking mutual benefit, valuing cooperation over competition, listening more, and staying in communication with our new teachers longer.

First, we create a win-win situation for mentors. Teachers are the best judge of effective instructional strategies and through the mentoring program are given the latitude of working together to enhance one another's skills. Our mentors grow professionally through reexamining their practices and beliefs. As the educational system struggles with restructuring and organizational shifts, the old bureaucratic style of supervision is in flux.

The new supervision is teacher-directed and collegial. For example, when one new teacher received a voice-mail message from a parent to call "immediately!" her mentor mischievously suggested that she return the call at midnight and say, "I just checked my messages. What's wrong? Has something happened?" This mentor's lighthearted response allowed the pair to have a good laugh and relaxed the new teacher before she called the parent. Offering the kind of assistance that the new teacher needs and wants is just one of many mentor roles (see Figure 2).

Second, we create a win-win situation for beginning teachers by helping them feel assisted and successful. During this transitional year from teacher training to the classroom, teachers experience a number of psychological shocks, including frustration, feelings of isolation, and lowered pupil expectations. Our program gives beginning teachers not only constructive criticism and feedback, but also help and encouragement. From brainstorming individual behavior plans in a special education classroom to solving special problems about techniques for playing in band, mentors interact with their beginning teachers in a variety of ways. After a beginning teacher observed her mentor's classroom many times during the first

Figure 2
Responsibilities of a Mentor

- Get involved in solving specific problems about curriculum, instruction, and relationships.
- Provide opportunities for classroom visits with feedback (beginning teacher's classroom, mentor's classroom, colleague's classrooms). Encourage visits to other classrooms by offering to cover the beginning teacher's classroom.
- Express positive feelings about teaching and help the beginning teacher attain those same feelings. Address the new teacher's thoughts about being a teacher.
- Help the new teacher cope with practical details of being a teacher.
- Assist with the new teacher's understanding and management of school authority.
- Listen to daily concerns, progress, and questions.
- Serve as a source of ideas.
- Be easily accessible, trustworthy, and understanding.
- Offer assistance on classroom management.
- Demonstrate professional competence.
- Help expand the beginning teacher's repertoire of teaching strategies.
- Show awareness of, commitment to, and familiarity with the new teacher's classroom.
- Schedule time willingly with the beginning teacher.
- Provide a task-oriented focus established through a two-way interchange about goals and procedures.

week of school, the mentor commented, "She took a lot of notes, and when I talked to her today, she says she still looks back at those notes for ideas and strategies."

What are the other win-win situations in our Beginning Teacher Mentor Program? Administrators find support from the mentors in their staff development efforts, students benefit by having a more confident beginning teacher, and parents are reassured that teachers are developing competencies and skills that are so essential to student learning. Finally, the entire school grows professionally. Teachers break out of their isolation as sharing ideas becomes central to continual improvement.

From Beginners to Professionals

The Beginning Teacher Mentor Program provides a means of increasing beginning teachers' productivity and commitment, thus preventing attrition. What separates new teachers from experienced professionals is not only the years of experience but also the knowledge and skills that experienced teachers develop over those years. A mentoring program structures a process for passing on this knowledge to beginning teachers in a systematic rather than a haphazard way. As a result, new teachers are more effective in their classrooms and more satisfied with their professional performance. One mentor remarked, "My praise lets her know that she is doing okay." Another liked being a "sounding board" for her beginning teacher, offering professional advice on how to handle situations with others. "My assistance in classroom organization and district guidelines and expectations helped minimize stress for my beginning teacher," said a third mentor.

Educators have long recognized the special needs of beginning teachers. Only recently, though, has the beginning-teacher role been equated with the first rung of a career ladder in which the teacher proceeds upward toward increasing levels of experience and proficiency. Because most career-ladder plans include a structured assistance program, a beginning-teacher mentor program utilizes the expertise of the experienced teachers to provide ongoing support and professional growth opportunities to enhance the skills and effectiveness of beginning teachers. During summer phone conversations, one mentor suggested to her beginning teacher that she take the district's guided reading class. The new teacher not only attended the class but also purchased the book on her own rather than wait for the first day of class. The facilitators and the mentor were impressed!

Our program is designed to promote the personal and professional well-being of beginning teachers, to transmit the culture of the school and the teaching profession, to improve teaching performance and student achievement, and to promote job-embedded staff development and the school as a learning community. Finally, with 30 percent of all beginning teachers leaving education within the first five years, increasing the retention of promising first-year teachers is the program's goal.

Learning Together

Although we usually focus professional development on formal inservice training, learning from one another in their daily interaction is probably the best way that teachers enhance their competence. Thus, the manner in which a new teacher acquires skills related to teaching, the type of skills needed, and the extent of skill development depend in large part on the school's prevailing norms and patterns of interaction.

The West Des Moines Community School District promotes norms of continual improvement and collegiality. We hold and support expectations that improving teaching is a collective rather than a solo enterprise and that analysis, evaluation, and experimentation—in concert with colleagues—set the conditions under which teachers become more effective. According to a mentor of both a first- and a second-year teacher, "When my mentees experience a high or a low, they seek me out. We celebrate or cry together, then create an action plan. Many times, the mentee has already shared an action plan in our previous conversation. We strengthen our bonds as we move through the school year."

In these ways, the Beginning Teacher Mentor Program encourages teachers to teach other teachers about teaching. In so doing, we assure our beginning teachers that they are qualified for—and supported in—the teaching profession.

Note

[1] Covey, S. (1989). *The seven habits of highly effective people: Powerful lessons in personal change*. New York: Simon & Schuster.

Mary Brooks is Site Coordinator for the Beginning Teacher Mentor Program, West Des Moines Community School District, 3550 George M. Mills Civic Parkway, West Des Moines, IA 50266 (e-mail: brooksm@wdm.k12.ia.us).

Mentoring the Mentors

Anne Coppenhaver and Laurel Schaper

By understanding adult learning theory, acquiring skills unique to mentoring, and identifying the characteristics of effective classrooms, experienced teachers in a Texas program prepare to assist their beginning colleagues and become better teachers themselves.

Few situations are as challenging as those experienced by first-year teachers, except perhaps trying to determine ways to support them. Novices must maneuver the minefield of disruptive students, mountains of paperwork, and mental and physical exhaustion. Mentors must help them be competent teachers while negotiating one new experience after another. State initiatives to support new teachers in California and to fund an induction-period mentoring program in Texas are just two examples of attempts to mitigate the difficulties that new teachers face.

As teacher attrition statistics demonstrate, not only do first-year teachers leave the profession, but experienced teachers are also exiting in droves. Too often, educators get stuck in the disillusionment phase, unable to see a light at the end of the tunnel. Unrejuvenated, they change careers, taking with them a wealth of knowledge and experience.

In August 1998, Region IV Educational Service Center, a consortium of 56 Texas Gulf Coast–area school districts, identified 1,000 unfilled full-time teaching positions, not including those in the metropolitan Houston Independent School District. With the attrition rate and new growth in the area, Region IV was projecting 7,200 teaching vacancies for the

Authors' note: The mentoring program was originally funded through a grant from the Texas Education Agency to the University of Houston-Clear Lake's School of Education to establish a pilot Center for Professional Development and Technology. Mentors for all teacher preparation candidates now participate in "Professional Mentoring to Enhance Classroom Instruction" as part of the commitment that UHCL makes to its public school partners.

1999–2000 school year. This is not an isolated story in one corner of Texas; it is a tale told across the nation.

One University's Answer

Five years ago, the University of Houston-Clear Lake (UHCL) began to restructure its teacher education program. Initially, mentors, prospective interns, and university faculty were hopeful that new and wonderful insights would develop as the result of offering a yearlong internship that went beyond the 12 weeks of traditional student teaching. The mentor teachers were eager to help, but they said quite clearly that they were unsure about their roles. The lead mentor teachers on each campus, our site coordinators, were insistent that we needed to provide resources for teachers who were mentoring these interns. "We can't just do the same old thing and expect different results. What *else* are we going to do to get our mentors prepared?" We have subsequently developed a mentoring program that meets the needs of school districts to initiate new teachers and to retain experienced ones.

Today, 25 professional development schools in 10 local school districts associated with UHCL are using the program with positive results. Texas City Independent School District has implemented the seminar we call "Enhancing Instructional Strategies Through Professional Mentoring" for its entire instructional staff. By policy, the district requires all mentor teachers to participate in this workshop. The rejuvenation of experienced teachers in this mentoring program was an unplanned bonus.

The Cry for Help

At the end of the first year of placing interns at our professional development schools, mentors were in dire need of help. They needed effective tools to help them with observation and feedback. University curriculum specialists and site coordinators discussed the matter for several months. A university specialist in needs assessment and systemic reform suggested that research literature on change might give the group direction.

Mentor teachers, however, had a bottom-line approach. They were not interested in theory alone. The information we identified to meet their needs is not usually considered part of curriculum practices, lesson planning, or instructional strategies. Instead, it is associated with the education of prospective principals. As developers, we were in unfamiliar territory, belonging to no one academic department of the School of Education. Mentor teachers were not fazed; they wanted access to supervisory tools so that they might help teachers improve. The idea that these skills might be difficult to teach did not matter a great deal to them.

Together, site coordinators and a new university faculty member stepped off the edge of our known world of curriculum and instruction and ventured into the unknown, combining classroom instructional expertise and supervisory responsibilities. We spent five days exploring how mentoring is different from teaching. Why is it different (and sometimes counterintuitive) from teaching youngsters? And, most important, how can mentors foster professional thinking? We carved out a three-day seminar in which mentors could share discoveries and practice skills.

The Familiar and the Unfamiliar

Many workshop activities help teachers recall what they already know so that they can apply that knowledge to mentoring. For instance, most teachers are well aware of their own learning styles and why they need to use this knowledge in their classrooms. Our guiding workshop question then became, Of what relevance is this knowledge to working with new teachers? When mentors provide resources and data about observations in a manner that supports the novice's preferred learning style, the tired tenderfoot can most clearly listen and understand.

We also wanted to refresh our acquaintance with the language of effective teaching so that mentors value talking about teaching in order to model thinking as a *teacher* thinks. In Texas, we have the shared professional experience of a state appraisal system across grade levels and school districts. The Professional Development and Appraisal System (PDAS) is a cogent, research-based framework that describes the learner-centered classroom. Therefore, we speak the language of this system and ask mentors to use what they already know to articulate our profession to novices.

The Look and Sound of Student Success

Using the language of the PDAS, workshop participants describe what activities they would see in a classroom if students were mastering instructional objectives. We examine microscopically what student success looks and sounds like in the classroom. If student learning is taking place, what is the teacher doing and what are the students doing? A lively discussion of several hours ensues as we question how an observer might detect student learning, how any experienced teacher might recognize it, and how we can share this process with our beginning colleagues.

We provide mentors with options for collecting data during observations that are simple, clear, and grounded in practical application. Suddenly, the light dawns as mentors realize that what they must observe and focus on is not what the novice does in the instructional setting, but whether the students are getting it. Are the students performing as expected? Are they learning?

Some workshop information is unfamiliar to many mentors. For instance, the concepts of helping adults learn must be coupled with knowledge of *how* adults learn. If an adult learns on a "need to know" basis, then mentors must first create or identify a situation for which novices need the new skill or knowledge. Then, mentor teachers must provide new teachers with the opportunity to solve problems independently. It is not necessary to lead adults by the hand as we do for some young learners. What is true for adult mentees is also true for their adult mentors. Until mentors understand the need, relevance, and importance of what is being shared, mentoring workshops are doomed to failure.

William Draves, in *How to Teach Adults* (1997), discusses four ways that adults are indeed different from youngsters in the classroom. Emotionally, adults come to any learning setting with more, not less, emotional background and a longer history of either success or failure than our young students do (p. 6). Teachers have often been successful learners in earlier settings, which usually makes them open to learning; they value it highly. However, they have also been used to being the leader, not only of their own learning, but also the leader of the learning of everyone around them. As learners, teachers need to be part of learning activities in which everyone leads, participates, and has important work to do.

Physically, mentally, and socially, adults are different from young students. The physical surroundings—including room temperature, seating comfort, and light and sound levels—are important to adults. Even young adults are attuned to, and distracted by, their physical setting when they are trying to learn. Therefore, for most teacher groups, paying attention to the room conditions and arrangements is an essential part of organizing so that everyone can learn.

Mentally, however, adults are a joy to teach. According to Draves, they are problem-oriented and concerned with specific topics of relevance to them (p. 9). This very readiness to learn, combined with the social characteristics of being experienced in the ways of the world, makes teaching adults a challenge. We can be sure that every teacher in the room will already have had an experience with mentoring, for example. They have been mentored, have mentored someone, and have some definite ideas about how to do it. As mentors of mentors, we must recognize these teacher experiences as abundant resources for resolving problems and making suggestions. "Teaching adults to learn, then, is not so much trying to convince, cajole, or tutor, as it is helping adults to learn" (p. 14).

"Thinking Like a Teacher"

Walking and talking like a teacher are only part of what mentors need to share about their profession. The heart of mentoring is supporting new educators so that they *think* as a teacher thinks. Our goal is to develop strong professionals who are ready to join other educators on the journey to student success.

But mentors need tools. We prepare them to observe classroom instruction and to reflect on teaching with novices in a conference setting. The process begins with, and depends heavily on, their ability to articulate the basic concepts of our profession. We include cognitive coaching, as explained in *Another Set of Eyes* (ASCD, 1988), to help explore these skills as well as to iterate the importance of fostering professional independence among new teachers. We also employ representative teaching episodes and samples of professional conferencing, such as those found in the videotape series *Effective Teaching Techniques* (Teacher Center Board, University of Houston-Clear Lake, 1987) and *A Guide to Prepare Support Providers for Work with Beginning Teachers* (Baron & Gless, 1996).

Honing Reflective Skills

Finally, we attack the biggest concern of most mentors: How do I tell my mentee what is happening in the classroom without hurting his or her feelings? Imagine the mentors' relief when we remind them that they are cognitive coaches and that the purpose of the observation is to provide the teachers with data so that they can make decisions about future lessons. Mentors are released from the oppressive, traditionally evaluative components of their supervisory role. They are elated to discover that they can serve as colleagues in the classroom, collecting data for new teachers on instructional and management strategies and helping them reflect on their teaching experiences.

Using the observational skills learned in the workshop, mentors provide their mentees with specific data that address effective teaching practices. The following examples of feedback from mentor teachers illustrate typical, noncritical information collected during an observation:

- 8:15 a.m. to 8:45 a.m.: More than 90 percent of students were actively engaged in the learning process.
- 9:45 a.m.: Students entered the classroom and immediately began working on the warm-up activity on the board. They demonstrated established procedures.
- After asking Chris to provide an example of a metaphor, you prompted him with two additional questions to assist him in arriving at the correct answer.
- You applied management rules consistently and fairly. You said to Julie, "I've asked that pens not be thrown in the classroom. That will be a learning choice."
- From 1:20 p.m. to 1:32 p.m., you addressed 11 questions to the entire class, resulting in a global response. Can you be sure that 100 percent of your students mastered the skill?
- During the 20-minute class discussion of pronouns, I noticed that you called at least 42 student names to answer questions. During that time, of the 24 students in your class, 4 students were able to respond accurately to your questions.

Mentors are often unsure about how to share the data. So we examine the mentor-mentee relationship across the stages of the preobservation conference, the observation, and the postobservation conference. Teachers remember that trust and rapport are important to any mentoring relationship. They devote time and a great deal of energy to generating banks of rich conference questions, using our language of effective teaching. We share our resources and rehearse the language until mentors are comfortable with phrases such as "research shows that" instead of "I want to see." With their colleagues, mentors craft and experiment with pertinent, guiding, open-ended questions.

We then practice, practice, and practice. Fully one-half of workshop time is devoted to mentors' using and honing newly learned skills. In groups of three, mentors participate in role-playing activities, assuming the roles of mentor, new teacher or intern, and monitor. They conduct conferences after observing videotaped staged lessons from which data are collected. The person in the mentoring role shares the data objectively with the mentee while a monitor observes the interaction and mirrors the language used.

Is the Program Working?

Since the program's inception in 1994, we have facilitated workshops for more than 850 teachers and administrators. Even today, the seminar remains dynamic and changes on the basis of feedback. Following each three-day seminar, workshop participants respond to six questions and statements. These comments provide a wealth of information about the desire of educators to mentor one another as well as novice teachers.

From Tyler to Brownsville, from Galveston to Goose Creek, Texas teachers relate that they develop insights into their own instructional and management techniques as well as those of novices. Some of our prompts, and the representative responses of participants, follow:

1. Discuss three things you learned during the workshop.
   - Communicating more effectively with other teachers
   - Cognitive coaching
   - Learning about my own work while observing someone else
   - The language of effective teaching

2. List two things that facilitated your learning.
   - Being able to practice our skills
   - Generating a question bank
   - Interaction with peers
   - Role playing
   - Concrete examples

3. Share one thing you plan to do with this new information.
   - Use the language learned in my own experiences
   - Buddy with another mentor and analyze different aspects of my own teaching
   - Be another set of eyes for my mentee and colleagues
   - Self-evaluate by using the Professional Development and Appraisal System domains and look for deficiencies in my own teaching
   - Utilize the choice-making process with my own students

4. As a district mentor, what would you like to accomplish before the end of the school year?
   - Remain in contact with the university supervisor so that I will be aware of changes in the program and will have access to new information that will help my intern and me
   - Interact with teachers at my school to share the experiences of the mentor-mentee relationship to help me see my own strengths and weaknesses
   - Participate in the pre- and postconference process and feel comfortable with my mentee
   - Learn to share and be more open to providing knowledge and experiences
   - Enhance my own skills as well as offer my time to others

On the basis of this representative sampling, we see that experienced teachers are learning skills to mentor new and preservice teachers. They are reminded of what constitutes student success in the classroom. This is not new information—they have always known it. Sometimes, however, beneath the weight of their other management responsibilities, experienced educators may neglect attention to student learning.

New teachers, experienced teachers in professional development schools, and their university faculty partners have traveled far on this collaborative mentoring journey. Novices benefit from learning how to "think like a teacher." Mentors are empowered to talk about teaching in reflective, noncritical ways. They teach novices to observe student learning and to reflect on the complex process we call teaching. University faculty members have a rare opportunity to participate in developing best practices for mentoring, a reflective union of academic theory and the realities of the public school classroom. The reflection engendered by the mentoring program ensures that the journey continues and that the voyage benefits all the travelers.

References

Association for Supervision and Curriculum Development. (1988). *Another set of eyes* (Videotape Series). Alexandria, VA: Author.

Baron, W., & Gless, J. (1996). *A guide to prepare support providers for work with beginning teachers*. Santa Cruz, CA: Santa Cruz New Teacher Project.

Draves, W. A. (1997). *How to teach adults* (2nd ed.). Manhattan, KS: The Learning Resources Network.

Teacher Center Board, University of Houston-Clear Lake. (1987). *Effective teaching techniques* (Videotape Series). Houston, TX: Author.

Anne Coppenhaver is Director of the Center for Educational Programs at the University of Houston-Clear Lake and a lecturer in Educational Administration. She can be reached at 2700 Bay Area Blvd, Houston, TX 77058 (e-mail: coppenhaver@cl.uh.edu). **Laurel Schaper** is the Site Coordinator for the Texas City Independent School District. She can be reached at 500 14th Ave. N., Texas City, TX 77590 (e-mail: schaperl@texascity.isd .tenet.edu).

Baltimore Takes Mentoring to the Next Level

Tom Ganser, Mary Jacqe Marchione, and Arlene K. Fleischmann

A systemwide Teacher Mentor Program focuses on teacher effectiveness, student achievement, and teacher longevity to support educational reform in urban schools—one classroom at a time, one teacher at a time.

Current research clearly links student achievement with teacher quality. Among the key factors associated with declining student performance are inadequate practical training and daily support for new teachers. According to a report of the National Commission on Teaching and America's Future (1996), teachers in the United States have more college education than their non-U.S. colleagues but fewer opportunities to share expertise with other teachers or to be guided by veteran teachers in the crucial first years of teaching. The lack of gradual, guided induction into teaching and the isolation that many beginning teachers experience cause them to develop undesirable coping mechanisms that thwart their effectiveness and diminish opportunities for meaningful student learning.

Support for New Teachers Is on the Rise

Systematic support for beginning teachers, often in the form of mentoring, has grown dramatically (Darling-Hammond & Sclan, 1996). The U.S. Department of Education (1998) reports that 51 percent of teachers with up to three years of teaching have participated in some form of induction activities. This figure compares with a participation rate of only 16.5 percent for teachers with 20 or more years of experience.

The importance of supporting beginning teachers will accelerate over the next decade as significant numbers of new teachers enter the profession because of population growth, a continuing wave of teacher retirements, and state and federal initiatives resulting in reduced class size.

Without assistance, many potentially good teachers become discouraged and reduce their commitment to teaching to a survival level or abandon the profession entirely (Gold, 1996; Huling-Austin, 1990).

The Teacher Mentor Program of Baltimore County Public Schools

Baltimore County Public Schools (BCPS), an urban school district with an enrollment of approximately 103,000 children, has charted an aggressive course of action to enhance the effectiveness of new teachers and to keep them in the profession.

In the past three years, BCPS has hired more than 2,500 new teachers, approximately one-third of the entire teaching force, because of population growth and teacher attrition. To address both this influx of inexperienced teachers and low student achievement, the district established the Teacher Mentor Program in 1996. The program supports teachers who are new to the district; have five or fewer years of experience; and are assigned to schools with low student achievement, a history of high teacher attrition, and a significant percentage of students participating in free or reduced meals.

Focusing on Instruction and Achievement

The Teacher Mentor Program gives new teachers intensive on-site assistance from full-time mentors in the areas of effective instruction, assessment, behavior management, and interpersonal communication as they relate to student success. The program uses a rigorous application and interview process to select mentors. Mentors are instructional generalists who do not participate in the appraisal process, although they observe instruction with administrators and are trained in giving teachers instructional feedback.

The primary goals of the Teacher Mentor Program are (1) to increase student achievement by improving teacher effectiveness and daily instruction and (2) to retain capable new teachers by increasing their satisfaction with their teaching experience. The program is aligned with national, state, and local standards for comprehensive professional development and emphasizes the transfer of content and pedagogical knowledge to new teachers through continual support in the classroom.

Program Design Features

In its third year, the Teacher Mentor Program has 122 full-time mentors in 62 schools at all levels. Mentors observe instruction to engage teachers in reflective dialogue focused on student learning and on the demonstration of that learning. They work with new teachers to "chunk down" the Baltimore County Public Schools Essential Curriculum into meaningful daily instruction and appropriate assessment to drive that instruction. Mentors frequently model lessons and assist teachers in planning and analyzing lessons as well as in implementing best practice. They guide teachers toward effective behavior management and regularly use resources to address systemwide goals. Through workshops and grade-level and faculty meetings, mentors enhance teachers' understanding of data analysis, performance-based instruction and assessment, and curriculum.

The Teacher Mentor Program is research-based and results-driven. A careful review of the literature by Howard Gardner, David Perkins, Linda Darling-Hammond, and others has focused all mentor initiatives on the following question: What is the impact of the Teacher Mentor Program on teacher effectiveness, student achievement, and teacher longevity? The answer continues to provide data for policymakers that support the fact that educational reform must occur in schools—one classroom at a time, one teacher at a time.

Mentor Training and Support

Monthly mentor-training sessions address the components of effective instruction, including the application of new knowledge, technical skills, and interpersonal skills. New mentors participate in supplemental training before they assume their responsibilities. The mentor as a lifelong learner is the embodiment of the most recent training that Baltimore County Public Schools offers in state and local assessment, the implementation of curriculum, the observation-feedback process, the use of technology to enhance instruction, the adult learner, behavior management, action research, and data analysis. A week of summer training highlights results-driven instruction, the characteristics of the new teacher, mentoring as a unique professional role, the Individuals with Disabilities Education Act (IDEA), reading instruction, and performance-based assessment.

In addition to using county resources in the Departments of Professional Development; Curriculum and Instruction; Special Education; and Research, Assessment, and Accountability, the Teacher Mentor Program invites national researchers and consultants such as Thomas Armstrong, Fred Jones, and Mike Schmoker to make presentations during mentor-training workshops throughout the year. To maintain a culture of learning and inquiry, mentors regularly participate in study groups and networking sessions. The program also provides mentors with *The Mentor Handbook*, an annually revised volume of research and effective instructional practices, and *The Mentor Newsletter*, which updates materials and resources.

Monitoring the Program

The school-based administrator and the BCPS Department of Professional Development collaboratively supervise the Teacher Mentor Program. Mentors are observed and evaluated according to the Baltimore County Public Schools Appraisal Process. An additional evaluation checklist, developed in consultation with the Department of Research, Assessment, and Accountability, aligns the mentor initiative with systemwide goals and the teacher evaluation form.

Program supervision ensures the transfer of new knowledge acquired during training to the school setting as a result of goal-setting conferences; observation and feedback; data collection and analysis; evaluation conferences; the effective use of resources; and continual support in instruction, assessment, management, and communication. In addition, school principals on special assignment furnish nonevaluative assistance and support to principals with five or fewer years of experience in schools served by mentors and in other low-achieving schools.

Program Results

Research on the effectiveness of the program has been ongoing since its inception in 1996–97. For example, from fall 1997 to spring 1998, mentors reported an overall positive increase in the performance of new teachers on 10 important aspects of effective instruction—from 56 percent of the teachers in the fall to 77 percent in the spring.

In a survey that new teachers completed in fall 1997 rating the assistance received from mentors in 13 areas, all but two of the service areas were rated positively by more than 90 percent of the teachers who believed that they needed those services. By spring 1998, more than 90 percent of the teachers wanting a given service rated positively all services but one, "models lessons," which was rated positively by 85 percent of the teachers wanting that service. With respect to teacher attrition, teacher attrition decreased 39 percent in the original 20 participating mentor schools in 1996–97.

To date, findings point to steady increases in student achievement in those schools receiving the services of mentors, as measured by standardized tests that include the Maryland School Performance Assessment Program (MSPAP), the Maryland Writing Test, and the Maryland Functional Math Test. For example, at the end of 1996–97, schools with mentors had 20 percent fewer 1st graders at or above grade level in reading as measured by the Word Identification Checklist than more affluent schools without mentors did. By the end of 1997–98, this gap was cut nearly in half among 2nd graders in the schools with mentors. Of the 10 middle schools receiving mentor services, 9 registered gains from 1996–97 to 1997–98 in the passing rate for the Maryland Writing Test.

BCPS regularly analyzes and compares the results of the MSPAP, the California Test of Basis Skills, the Gates McGinitie Reading Test, and functional tests in schools receiving the services of mentors with data from schools not assigned mentors. Additional qualitative and quantitative data that are collected and analyzed include mentor journals describing observed outcomes and the impacts of the Teacher Mentor Program; individual and focus-group interviews with mentors, new teachers, and principals; and the results of selected school assessments and program-specific instruments.

In 1998–99, the addition of approximately 15,000 checklists completed monthly by the mentors ("How Are the Teachers Doing?") and by the new teachers to whom they are assigned ("How Have the Mentors Helped You?") has enhanced research on the effectiveness of the Teacher Mentor Program. In addition, researchers study the impact of mentoring on teacher effectiveness, student achievement, and teacher longevity and examine program strengths and needs.

Moving Mentoring Beyond Emotional Support and Help with Paperwork

The state superintendent of Maryland and the National Staff Development Council have recognized the Teacher Mentor Program as a state and national model for new-teacher training and induction. We attribute the success of the program to many factors that educational leaders responsible for the design and implementation of formal mentoring programs for new teachers should consider.

A thorough review of research on mentoring and mentoring programs as a form of staff development—especially the selection, preparation, and support of mentors (Ganser, 1996)—informed the initial design of the Teacher Mentor Program. Baltimore County Public Schools delegated leadership of the program to professional development specialists whose commitment is reflected in unabashed advocacy at the local, state, and national levels.

From the start, Baltimore County Public Schools decided to create a program that extends beyond simply providing new teachers with emotional support and help with procedural matters to offering a comprehensive program whose ultimate success—and accountability—lies in enhancing teacher effectiveness to improve student achievement. In this regard, BCPS intentionally designed the Teacher Mentor Program to support its systemwide goal of "Student Achievement: First Things First."

Integrating the Teacher Mentor Program

Program developers made efforts to ensure that the Teacher Mentor Program does not exist, and is not perceived by district administrators and teachers, as a separate program for new teachers that is disconnected from other staff development efforts. This inherent problem in formal mentoring programs often goes unaddressed (Ganser, 1999). For instance, because mentors work with several new teachers in one school, the school's staff view the mentors as members of the staff rather than as outsiders who periodically appear. As one mentor commented, "I am recognized, welcomed, and feel part of this staff."

Comments from principals suggest that the influence of mentors extends beyond the new teachers in the school to all the teachers. For example, one principal said, "The mentor is very valuable and willing to give us suggestions on what we can all do to improve instruction." Another principal noted, "The mentor is working to help us all with how we do assessment." Even the children view the mentors as one of their teachers. "After I did a demonstration class," reported a mentor, "the kids said to me, 'When are you coming back? We really like it when you are here.'"

An additional benefit of the Teacher Mentor Program lies in its role in fostering leadership development in the teachers who participate as new teachers or as mentors. For example, a 5th grade teacher writes,

> I began my career as a 5th grade teacher two years ago. I was soon feeling overwhelmed with the demands placed on me as a new teacher. I was excited about beginning my career, and I wanted to be the best I could be in the classroom. My mentor began to offer the help that would turn things around. She taught me to work smart as well as hard.
>
> I do not know where I would be as an educator if it were not for my mentor's consistent efforts to help me meet the seemingly endless challenges facing a new teacher. As I enter the third year of my career, I have been asked to serve as the grade-level chair for the 5th grade team. This is a challenge I can embrace. My mentor has helped me develop a level of independence and self-confidence that enables me to live up to the high expectations placed on me as a teacher.

Since the Teacher Mentor Program began, approximately 25 mentors have assumed other leadership positions in Baltimore County Public Schools, including assistant principalships, central office positions, and university assistantships. Naturally, they carry to their new work their knowledge and experiences about the perceived and actual needs of new teachers, the stages of teacher development, and what it feels like to be a new teacher in Baltimore County Public Schools.

The Baltimore County Public Schools Teacher Mentor Program demonstrates that assisting new teachers can extend beyond asking "How's it going?" over a cup of coffee to enhancing teacher effectiveness and improving student achievement. The Teacher Mentor Program creates a creditable win-win situation for teachers, for administrators, and, especially, for the children whom they serve.

References

Darling-Hammond, L., & Sclan, E. M. (1996). Who teaches and why: Dilemmas of building a profession for the twenty-first century. In J. Sikula, T. J. Buttery, & E. Guyton (Eds.), *Handbook of research on teacher education* (2nd ed.) (pp. 67–101). New York: Macmillan.

Ganser, T. (1996). Preparing mentors of beginning teachers: An overview for staff developers. *Journal of Staff Development, 17*(4), 8–11.

Ganser, T. (1999, March). Enhancing new teacher mentoring programs. *NASSP Practitioner, 25*(3), 1–4.

Gold, Y. (1996). Beginning teacher support: Attrition, mentoring, and induction. In J. Sikula, T. J. Buttery, & E. Guyton (Eds.), *Handbook of research on teacher education* (2nd ed.) (pp. 548–594). New York: Macmillan.

Huling-Austin, L. (1990). Teacher induction programs and internships. In W. R. Houston (Ed.), *Handbook of research on teacher education* (pp. 535–548). New York: Macmillan.

National Commission on Teaching and America's Future. (1996). *What matters most: Teaching for America's future*. Woodbridge, VA: Author.

U.S. Department of Education, Office of Educational Research and Improvement. (1998). *Toward better teaching: Professional development in 1993–94*, NCES 98-230. Washington, DC: Author.

Tom Ganser is Director of the Office of Field Experiences, University of Wisconsin-Whitewater, 800 West Main St., Whitewater, WI 53190 (e-mail: gansert@uwwvax.uww.edu). **Mary Jacqe Marchione** is Director of the Department of Professional Development, Baltimore County Public Schools, 600 Stemmers Run Rd., Baltimore, MD 21221 (e-mail: mmarchione@bcps.org). **Arlene K. Fleischmann** is Coordinator of the Department of Professional Development, Baltimore County Public Schools, 600 Stemmers Run Rd., Baltimore, MD 21221.

"I Am SO Excited!" Mentoring the Student Teacher

Anna K. Schriever

When mentor teachers view their work as research in progress, they grow along with beginning educators.

> I'm so excited! I can't wait to get into the classroom!
>
> —Miss Smith

> From the time I first began school, I just knew I wanted to be a teacher. Now, after three and one-half years of studying, I finally get to teach.
>
> —Miss Jones

Remember the excitement, the exhilaration, of finally having your own class? It's the first day of school, only better, because you've attained your goal—you're the teacher. I have relived that feeling 12 times in the last eight years as I had the privilege of mentoring 12 student teachers at the beginning of their careers. Their vibrant enthusiasm is contagious, and I was that way, too. But as they settle into the routines of the classroom, the realities of the awesome job intrude. The student teachers experience the paperwork. They consider the curriculum and the proficiencies to be mastered. They encounter the heavy responsibilities, and many student teachers become overwhelmed. "How do you do it all?" they ask. Then we, as master teachers, begin to teach them our craft.

Schools are transforming the educational paradigm. Districts need to increase test scores and to improve attendance. Teachers are trying to change the way they teach and to become the best teachers possible. However, the "connecting of schooling and the educating of new teachers have virtually guaranteed that the status quo would be protected; tomorrow's teachers are mentored by today's" (Goodlad, 1990, p. 185).

The logical place to change the schools is not in the schools themselves, but in the university teacher preparation programs. What changes are being made in these programs?

Teaching in a Midwestern university town provides many opportunities for me to improve my own teaching and to inspire that of future teachers. My classroom is often observed and recorded, and it's one in which both students and faculty participate. For the last eight years of my teaching career, I have supervised at least one and as many as three student teachers each year. Some have been excellent; some have been mediocre; one was unsuccessful; and one was unprofessional. Even with all this experience, I have had no formal coursework on mentoring student teachers. My mentoring followed a handout from Midwest U. and the advice from university supervisors.

An Insider's Research on Mentoring

My philosophy for preparing student teachers is, "You cannot learn to teach without teaching." So as soon as possible, I let each student teacher teach the class. When student teachers experienced problems, we worked together to solve them. I often felt frustrated: I don't agree with what she's doing with my children. I want my class back. I would ask myself questions: Am I doing this right? What could I be doing better? I wanted to improve my mentoring. So I began an action research project to improve it. By action research, I mean insider research, research that is meaningful to my classroom situation. As an action researcher, I identify concerns, conduct research, refine suggestions, and reflect upon them.

First, I read research done by others. Surfing the Internet, I found a reading list from a course for supervising teachers. I went to Midwest U.'s library and found some articles on the list. As I read through them, I noticed that several innovations repeated themselves. Among these were the use of technology (computers, video cameras, and tape recorders); professional development schools; and reflective journals. Using the computer would be great, and we could try taping, both on audio and video. Midwest University has a professional development school for training student teachers, but my school was not part of it. Maintaining reflective journals and recording seemed the place to start.

Beatie (1995) suggests that "when student teachers and cooperating teachers can engage in inquiry and reflection necessary to challenge their practices and change the stereotypes of teaching and learning that currently exist, they can overcome obstacles to reform'" (p. 53). Gipe and Richards (1992) say that "supervisors should urge prospective teachers to think reflectively about their work . . . and to keep journals" (p. 52). They say that research supports the value of a journal as a vehicle to promote and document reflective thinking. Although reflection does not necessarily improve teaching, there is evidence that student teachers who participate in reflective teaching programs rather than traditional programs are "less anxious about teaching, and they are more able to think and talk about teaching and learning" (p. 53). So I accepted reflection as a valuable part of the student teaching experience and decided that both my student teacher and I ought to be doing more of it.

Maintaining Reflective Journals

I began to keep a daily journal of classroom events and observations of Miss Smith, an eight-week student teacher. What is the best way to be a good observer? Barker and Desrochers (1992) suggest several techniques: recording interactions with students, recording levels of questioning, recording movement patterns of the teacher, and using script taping. While observing Miss Smith, I used a seating chart to record her oral interaction with students. To record levels of questioning, I used Bloom's Taxonomy. This list encourages teachers to ask both literal-recall questions of direct knowledge and those of the higher orders of thinking, such as analysis, comparison, and evaluation. I used script taping, an actual written account of a lesson, and recorded interaction between the students and the teacher. These observations helped me collect data, which helped me communicate more effectively with Miss Smith.

I immediately noticed the children responding well to the various activities she planned. On February 25, Miss Smith wrote in her journal,

> They really liked reading along with me as I read the story *Down By the Bay* to them. I chose to make a mural together about the book, rather than following our original idea of having them draw pictures individually. The kids thought about the story song more and about the silly rhymes that could work as a result of making the mural.

She was right; the children loved the book so much that they continued to choose that story to read at free reading.

On February 28, I wrote in my journal,

> As I thought about today, I realized that Miss Smith had not actually taught anything at all. She merely gave out and explained worksheets. Is this the example I gave her?

More than just describe and observe her lessons, I was beginning to reflect: Had I modeled these lessons?

Modeling Effective Instruction

One suggestion in the supervising guidelines is to model for your student teacher. Daniel Martin (1997) writes, after 18 months of research on mentoring preservice teachers,

> Teaching is shaped according to the models of cooperating teachers. As student teachers borrow routines they are not merely mimicking, but rather making an attempt to research into one's own pedagogy the fit between the routine and how one wished to teach. (p. 193)

I thought I had modeled lessons. Obviously the modeling step needed more direction. Barker and Desrochers (1992) advise, "After the student teacher observes . . . teaching techniques, explain what was done as well as why it was done" (p. 23). They also suggest that copying the teacher "provides a smoother transition and should be followed with originality and experimentation in teaching" (p. 24). I had missed the copying step and had expected the originality.

I questioned other cooperating teachers to see how they began coaching student teachers. I discovered that one teacher used a lesson plan format and the student observed the teacher. Then, they discussed the lesson together, talking about the parts of a good lesson: What did you think of the opening? Could you state the objectives? Which of the activities were the most successful? Did you notice the way the lesson was closed? My colleague felt that discussion led to the natural steps of critiquing. Observing me allowed Miss Smith to think about a lesson without the pressures of performance. Another student teacher said, "I think being able to observe someone teaching each subject before I teach it will be a great asset. It'll give me a chance to see how each subject is handled."

As I talked to colleagues about my project, I uncovered typical problems at all grade levels. Several teachers said that the students didn't know how to teach reading. Their lesson plans weren't complete. They didn't know how to include all components of a lesson—from introduction to closure. These statements mirrored my own ideas. When I asked other mentor teachers how they handled lessons plans, I received several worthy suggestions. One was to write the plan and have the student teacher teach from it, another version of modeling. Another teacher said,

> Talk to the university supervisor about requiring the student teachers to use a specific format for writing lessons. Every supervisor does not require the same format and this makes it hard to know what preparation the students have had.

The Power of Observation

One day I wrote, "The children were rowdy, loud, whiny, argumentative, and easily distracted. Are they just testing her as an adult in control?" What could I do about it? Helping my student teacher solve discipline problems required more thinking. As I spoke with other cooperating teachers about their experiences, I discovered that we all had similar problems supervising our student teachers. My colleagues suggested the explanation could be in the attitude that the student teacher had toward the children. As one teacher said, "She fluctuated from being too friendly to being too stern. . . . She didn't provide the children with consistency."

In an article about professional development schools by Corinne Mantle-Bromley (1998), I found a brief discussion of this problem: "(A) teacher candidate, John, says, students treat him as if he were one of them" (p. 48). The solution for John was offered in a study group: "You're treating them (the students) too informally. You need to assert yourself in your language. . . . Speech and gestures may have sent unintentional messages to the students" (p. 48). Taking these ideas into consideration, I began to observe Miss Smith for consistency in her discipline and for assertive words, actions, and behaviors.

My journal was also a means to document Miss Smith's improvement in lesson planning and teaching methods. When she took over the full-time teaching load, we began a conversational journal in which we wrote to each other every day. On March 5, I wrote:

> The children enjoyed mixing the cookies. You were very brave to try it!
> I have some suggestions: Print out the recipe on a chart. Have some activities that they can do at the tables; for example, count chips on cookies and write how many, make a paper cookie, or write a sentence about cookies and draw a picture. It was a great idea—think through the lesson and keep all the kids involved.

Miss Smith responded:

> I was really excited about how well the children did with the chocolate chip cookie math. They were interested and seemed to understand what was going on addition- and subtraction-wise. The theme connecting everything together made transitions easier.
> Timmy was fascinated by making the cookies. I had never thought of the fact that some of the children may never have seen their parents make something from scratch.
> One thing I need to do is have something to keep the other children busy while I am working with a few of them at a time. Their attention spans are just too short to sit still and watch for that long.

Miss Smith made a good analysis of her lesson. She was aware of the children's attention span and modified her afternoon lesson accordingly. When the time came to write Miss Smith's evaluation, I had many specific areas of improvement about which to write. I could read back and find problem areas and discuss how she solved the problems. I knew that my student teacher had experienced growth.

Another benefit of my action research project was the way I became connected to other teachers. I became a "resident expert." Other teachers wanted to know what I had discovered. When I talked about the value of keeping a journal, one teacher offered suggestions. Some teachers who had taken a mentoring course offered to assist me in my research. They shared a particularly helpful manual by James B. Rowley (1993), which had some good suggestions for focusing journal writing and for observing. Other teachers asked for suggestions to help their student teachers. We began to build a community of practitioners. My colleagues and I decided to meet to improve student teachers' experiences.

Tools for Collaboration

The greatest benefit, though, was that writing in a journal became a tool for collaboration with student teachers. We became connected to one another through this special form of communication. As we wrote, we began to build another dimension of community. The conversational journal allowed us to write about the day, ask questions, reflect, and read about the same experience from two perspectives. A mentor's knowledge and expertise cannot be transferred completely to another person. You can only model after another and integrate what you like best into your own style.

Teaching is a lonely profession. Martin (1997) says, "It is idiosyncratic and is learned by oneself" (p. 194). Teachers can go for hours without talking to another adult. I learned about teaching by trial and error. Miss Smith left my class after eight weeks, only to return often—to see the children, but also to discuss concerns with her second assignment and to see what we were doing in the classroom. I found myself asking her for her opinions and suggestions about lessons. We had grown to trust and respect each other. Our journal helped us build a closer, more supportive relationship.

Miss Smith completed her eight-week assignment just two weeks before Miss Jones began. I reflected on lessons learned. Maintaining journals promoted collaboration, communication, and reflection. Detailed observation established a positive relationship, allowing constructive criticism. Modeling needed more direction. The following year, two teachers and I would form a discussion group to assist one another in mentoring. Would I continue keeping conversational journals? Yes, I would.

When Miss Jones joined my class, we started the conversational journal. I noticed that she was diffident about her teaching ability. I used the journal to offer her support and encouragement.

When I was absent, she wrote:

> The afternoon class went better, I think, because I had already done it once. . . . I adapted my lesson to fix some of the things that didn't work. I like being able to learn from my mistakes and being able to use that knowledge immediately. . . .The hardest part of the day was all the little stuff I had to remember—attendance, passing out papers, good notes, whose turn it was on the computer, assignments, remembering who had trouble with certain things. I was exhausted, but I was very excited. I got to teach.

References

Barker, G. P., & Desrochers, C. G. (1992). A head start for student teachers. *Executive Educator,* 14(5), 23–24.

Beatie, M. (1995). New prospects for teacher education: Narrative ways of knowing

teaching and teacher learning. *Educational Research*, 37(1), 53–69.
Gipe, J. P., & Richards, J. (1992). Reflective thinking and growth in novices' teaching abilities. *Journal of Educational Research*, 86(1), 52–54.
Goodlad, J. (1990). Better teachers for our nation's schools. *Phi Delta Kappan*, 72(3), 184–194.
Mantle-Bromley, C. (1998, February). "A day in the life" at a professional development school. *Educational Leadership*, 55(5), 48–51.
Martin, D. (1997). Mentoring in one's own classroom: An exploratory study of context. *Teaching and Teacher Education*, 13(2), 183–195.
Rowley, J. B. (1993). Mentoring in a helping-relationship program. Unpublished manuscript.

Anna K. Schriever is a kindergarten teacher. She may be reached at 326 E. Union St., Liberty, IN 47353 (e-mail: schreve1@si-net.com).

How to Help a New Teacher by Being a Buddy

Annette Ehrlich Lakein

When the new teachers at Charles E. Smith Jewish Day School said that they didn't know to whom they should turn for help, their veteran colleagues responded by becoming buddies.

While checking on the progress of her own students, Marsha Roman listens to the shouting and the noise of chairs being thrown in the room next door. Harriet Jones, the teacher in that room, is new this year. Marsha vividly remembers the hard time she had at the beginning of her teaching career and wants to help, but she does not know how to approach Harriet. At the end of the day, hoping for an opening, Marsha casually asks her, "How are things going? My students seemed restless today." Harriet replies, "Fine. The students were a little lively, but I like things lively."

The conversation is over.

David Calder, now in his fifth month of teaching, has graded his 10th grade English class's essay assignment. As David returns the assignment to his students, Martin Slipe calls out that his parents will be very unhappy with the grade that he received. Sure enough, the next day David hears from Mr. Slipe, Martin's father, who tells David that he has read the essay again and does not understand the grade his son received. Because Mr. Slipe writes professionally and helped his son with the essay, he knows that this is good writing.

After David explains his goals for the assignment and what Martin would need to do to improve his performance, Mr. Slipe announces that clearly David does not know the subject matter and does not understand children. In addition, he informs David that he has already joined a group of parents concerned about the lack of good teaching in the schools—he is sure that David has read about this in the newspaper. At his group's next meeting, Mr. Slipe will be discussing his dissatisfaction with the English department.

David hangs up the phone and stares into space.

An Unanswered Need

Harriet and David are two of many new teachers who have made the commitment to teach, not for high salaries or prestige, but because they enjoy working with teenagers and they want to make a difference. However, they may leave teaching because they feel isolated and powerless. They have not yet invested many years in the profession of teaching, and their commitment pales in comparison with the problems that they are facing. They do not feel secure in what they are doing and do not yet see the extent to which they have been successful. Bureaucracy, complaints, difficult assignments and schedules, insufficient materials, and often relocation to a new community are issues that they face.

In a high school setting, a department chair is responsible for helping a new teacher implement specific curriculum and instructional techniques in his or her discipline. A mentor teacher can do this as well. Both have the ability and the right to enter a classroom, meet with a new teacher, and provide the technical support that a teacher needs to make the transition from university to teaching.

The teachers at Charles E. Smith Jewish Day School have had good support from the administration and within the individual departments. But at a teacher book-group meeting, we discovered that the teachers who had joined our faculty that year still felt lost. They needed and wanted something more than the curricular and instructional support that they were getting. They needed friends with whom they could have coffee on a regular basis, feel safe and say anything on their minds, risk discussing new ideas and changes that they wanted to make in their classroom, and share their successes and failures without worrying about supervision and evaluation. The difficulty for a new teacher, they said, is not knowing whom to trust and whom to ask for help.

Old Fears, New Solutions

To provide our new teachers with the support that they need, our program pairs every new teacher with a veteran teacher. We don't want to confuse the role of the buddy with the role of the department chair, and we want to maintain confidentiality. What does the program look like? During the summer, a veteran teacher is paired with a new teacher, and a buddy pair is made. The administration provides information on the backgrounds, interests, and perceived needs of the new teachers; as the coordinator, I match the buddies, making sure that the veteran teacher and the new teacher are from different disciplines. An added benefit is the opportunity for new teachers to meet and work with teachers from other disciplines.

The experienced teacher will be one of a group of veterans who will be at the new teacher's side when he or she needs support during the year. Veteran teachers call their buddies and run the new-teacher orientation at Charles E. Smith Jewish Day School before the school year begins. During the orientation, the new teachers are introduced to the administration and staff, the academic calendar, the daily workings of our school, the student rules and procedures, the faculty requirements, and the evaluation procedures and parent-communication opportunities. They learn about our technology and library resources.

Together, the buddies consider how they will set a business-like tone for the year. They also tour the school campus and have time to sit and chat and eat and get to know one another informally. New teachers have often commented that because teachers run the orientation, with the support of the administration, they get a sense of well-being in joining our faculty. We welcome our new teachers at the beginning of the year, and we continue to provide regular meetings, both formally and informally, to avoid any feelings of isolation.

Eight times during the year, the veteran teacher–new teacher buddies meet as a structured group to discuss parent communication, classroom management, special student populations, parent-conference days, back-to-school days, student reports, and the school calendar. These meetings give new teachers time to ask questions in a safe environment.

Periodically, I send out anonymous questionnaires to survey what needs we have met and what needs we need to address. Different groups of teachers have different needs. Some years, the meetings focus on only nuts-and-bolts issues and explanations of our school's culture. Other years, the teachers want discussions that relate to what is happening in their classrooms. From my anonymous surveys, I discover that the new teachers continue to need someone who is experienced not only in classroom management, but also in negotiating the lines of communication in the school community.

Answering Questions, Easing Concerns

What is the veteran teachers' informal role early in the year? They must create a safe place for the new teacher and reduce the anxieties of the first weeks and months in a new environment. Questions at the beginning of the year are usually of a procedural nature, and the buddies meet frequently. As the new teachers acclimate to the school and the students, they begin to set up their own communication links within the school, and the buddies meet less often.

A set of verbs gives the best picture of what a veteran teacher does: *listen, coach, sponsor, push, challenge,* and then *listen more*. Our stated goal is to help each new teacher integrate into our school community quickly and learn how to work with our students and parents. We are facilitators for someone else's success.

Unexpected Benefits

Over the years, the program has grown, and we have discovered that the veterans have gained much. The veteran teachers enjoy working with the new teachers in an informal atmosphere. They no longer feel isolated; the collegiality of working as a team with other veterans and sharing the lives of new teachers each year has led to increased enthusiasm about themselves as teachers.

In addition, teachers coming into our school with fresh eyes often see needs that we no longer see. For example, because of the new-teachers' suggestions, we now hang a daily schedule in the office. We have also clarified the lines of communication and the chain of command. Even more, as each group of new teachers become veteran teachers, we have become a community.

As for Harriet, the new teacher in the first example, she has someone whom she can invite into her classroom to help her figure out how to establish order, and she can go into other classrooms to see how her students act and how other teachers manage their classes. She has someone to go to when she doesn't know what to ask but knows that something is wrong, and she knows that she will get help. Harriet is in control of her professional growth. David can role-play with his buddy before he gets back on the phone with this or any other parent. With his buddy, he will work on what his next step will be. Both teachers will continue to work with their department chairs; both will be part of all curricular teams. Their buddies will continue to work alongside them, being their best friends.

Annette Ehrlich Lakein is an English teacher and the buddy program coordinator at Charles E. Smith Jewish Day School, 11710 Hunter's Lane, Rockville, MD 20852 (e-mail: aelakein@umd5.umd.edu).

Get on the Team: An Alternative Mentoring Model

Randall L. Turk

In mentoring teams, everyone benefits: Novice teachers receive support from multiple mentors, and mentor teachers experience less stress and grow professionally with their colleagues.

Fourteen years ago, I decided to make a career change and enter the education profession after 20 years as an Air Force pilot. The teaching load was not what I had expected—five classes of 25 to 30 students, with four different preparations each day. In fact, many times I thought about returning to my previous career as a pilot. For me, my mentor made the difference between my remaining in the classroom and leaving it forever.

I was grateful then for my mentor's guidance; I remain grateful today because I would not have made it without her support. Reflecting back, I often ask myself, What benefit did my mentor receive for her effort and time? I know that this is a rhetorical question—she gained the satisfaction of helping a new teacher. She, like all good teachers, is naturally caring and supportive. But is there an even better way to reap the benefits of mentoring while reducing stress for all involved? The valuable lessons that I learned as a new teacher enhanced my ability to lead others through a new mentoring process—mentoring teams.

New-Teacher Stress

Teaching is more complex today than ever. Students come to school with problems that were not even imaginable 10 years ago. In addition to expecting teachers to deal with the increased complexity of student needs, administrators often ask them to become actively involved in school improvement. The expectation to do more in a complex setting has resulted in greater stress for the teacher.

Schools, K–12, are not the only places where the stress level has increased. The pace of life outside school has increased rapidly. We are so busy with daily routines that we have little time to reflect on the past or to consider the future. Bertman (1998) calls this phenomenon *hyper culture:* "High-speed living enforces a live-for-the-present mentality that obscures history and memory" (p. 18). By performing at warp speed, we disengage from the past and plunge toward the future so quickly that we are blind to what lies ahead. Teachers, like many other professionals, no longer have a place to hide or to seek refuge from the stressful workplace.

Many teachers leave the profession because they are stressed or have experienced burnout. Friedman (1995) defines *burnout* as the syndrome that occurs when an individual perceives a significant discrepancy between effort and results. Teachers who work long hours and see few results are prime candidates for leaving the education profession. They believe that their hard work and sacrifice are not being rewarded with positive outcomes.

Teachers leaving the profession early in their careers contribute to a shortage of qualified personnel. The effect is long-term as well as immediate. If a teacher with five years of experience leaves the classroom today, we lose the potential of having, in five years time, a 10-year veteran teacher. The continued loss of new teachers seriously drains expertise in a field in which experience is important. As a result, student learning suffers. Recognizing this problem, many school districts have instituted programs and policies to retain a valuable asset. Among these have been mentoring programs for new teachers.

Goals of Mentoring Programs

Mentoring is designed to provide the beginning teacher with peer support to help cope with the daily challenges of teaching. Odell and Ferraro (1992) state the three goals of mentoring: to provide guidance and support, to promote professional development, and to increase retention.

As a new teacher 14 years ago, I received immeasurable guidance and support from my mentor. Many days, I found myself questioning my teaching strategies and asking how to accomplish certain tasks. My mentor always took time to answer those questions and to offer support.

But mentoring, in many ways, is heavily weighted as a one-way relationship. Should we, as members of a stressful profession, expect a person to endure a one-way relationship that requires expending much time and energy? Experienced teachers will continue to mentor and be supportive of beginning teachers because they are caring individuals. But through reciprocal, collegial teaming, new teachers can get the same kind of mentor support while experienced teachers can share the responsibility and support one another in the process.

An Alternative Mentoring Model

Teams offer opportunities for individuals to work together in a mutually supportive environment. As a member of a team of primarily experienced teachers, a new teacher receives mentoring not from one person but from three or four people. At the same time, mentors receive support from all the team members, opening up opportunities to build trust and to discuss things that matter. Champy (1997), in discussing relationships within organizations, says that we need conversation, not communication. People need a climate in which they can share in two-way conversations and not be solely recipients of one-way communication.

If a team is to provide effective mentoring, it must be a *working team.* Dumaine (1994) defines working teams as those that accomplish daily work, have stable membership, and are self-led. Stable membership is essential for maintaining the important element of trust. But trust, the glue of relationships, takes time to grow and must begin with self-trust (Marshall, 1995). Trust among team members is the foundation for building caring relationships, and a set of caring relationships is a common element of successful teams (Powers, 1996).

Mentoring teams must also possess high performance standards. Katzenbach and Smith (1993) categorized the various levels of team performance as pseudo, potential, real, or high performance. High-performance teams have an established purpose and are committed to a common working approach. The members have complementary skills and are individually and mutually accountable. Each member is committed to the personal growth and success of the other members.

Teams As Mentors

Mentoring is a complex task that requires the mentor to assume myriad roles. In traditional mentoring programs, one person must assume all these roles and tasks. In a teaming environment, several members with various skills and expertise can assume mentoring roles, thereby broadening the support that they give to the beginning teacher. The transition from the traditional one-on-one model to a team model of mentoring requires systemic change. Changing to team mentoring like any other change, calls for individuals to adopt new behaviors and to assume ownership for new roles.

Reflecting on my early experiences as a new teacher, I can visualize the benefit of mentoring by teams. My mentor would have been able to share some of her mentoring responsibilities with other math department team members. A team format would have reduced her stress and allowed her to grow professionally. In addition, I would have gained different perspectives from other staff members. The greatest gain, perhaps, would have come from our professional discussions. As Robbins and Finley (1995) remind us, "The easiest and fastest way to learn is from other people. Without other people, the old wheel must be reinvented again and again and again" (p. 18).

During my first year of principalship, our school used the traditional model of mentoring. We experienced the usual problems—limited opportunity for discussion and high levels of stress. The next year, when we implemented academic or working teams by grade level, the mentoring process changed. Teams assumed the mentoring role even though the traditional procedures from the previous year were unchanged. All team members accepted responsibility for the new teacher on their team. They believed it was their role to guide the new teacher through problems and issues. The teams, by expanding their roles, improved the productivity of new teachers and moved us closer to the goal of student achievement.

Our academic mentoring teams gave the new teachers guidance and support in dealing with student academic and behavior issues. Each team met periodically to discuss students who were not achieving academic outcomes or were causing discipline problems in the classroom. The dialogue among team members allowed new and experienced teachers alike to help one another better meet each student's needs. The academic team frequently met with students and their parents to discuss academic and behavioral issues. Parents became partners in resolving students' problems.

By working with the academic team, the student, and the student's parents, new teachers had a support system to get through difficult situations. They became part of the corrective process without assuming complete responsibility. They were able to learn from experienced teachers and thus felt less stressed. In addition, new teachers became partners with their team members and the process helped to develop their self-esteem and self-confidence.

My research in two schools revealed the value that new teachers place on team mentoring. A teacher in a suburban junior high school of 1,350 students stated that being a member of an academic team was a tremendous help. She said that during her first two years of teaching, her team members provided a lot of mentoring: "It is like having three mentors" (Turk, 1994, p. 121). The other team members noted that mentoring helped them all develop a strong working relationship. A teacher at a rural middle school echoed their remarks: "As a first-year teacher, teaming really helped me and kept the stress down" (Turk, p. 154).

The teams at both schools are self-led and empowered to make decisions normally reserved for administrators. For instance, teams deal directly with issues of student discipline; they make recommendations either for expulsion or for changing the core subject schedule to meet their students' unique needs.

Mentoring the Mentor

The pace of today's hyper culture places great emphasis on the present at the expense of reflection and consideration of the future (Bertman, 1998). This stressful environment accentuates the need for mentors to receive support and mentoring from their peers. As Herman and Gioia (1998) state, individuals need to know how they make an impact on the overall mission of an organization. An individual's feelings and emotions are important elements for job satisfaction and for making meaning of work. Open communication, according to Ralston (1995), allows coworkers to deal with their feelings and emotions: "When negative energy is suppressed, so too is positive energy" (p. 9).

By coordinating team members to act as mentors together, we let experienced teachers share the responsibility of mentoring while receiving benefits from a collaborative relationship. The mentor should be mentored and grow with beginning and fellow experienced teachers.

Every relationship provides an opportunity for individuals to grow and improve together. Team members who assume roles to help others improve inherently assume roles for self-improvement. The mentoring team provides opportunities for all members to grow professionally and excel in the classroom.

References

Bertman, S. (1998). Hyper culture. *The Futurist, 32*(9), 16–23.

Champy, J. A. (1997). Preparing for organizational change. In F. Hesselbein, M. Goldsmith, & R. Beckhard (Eds.), *The organization of the future* (pp. 9–16). San Francisco: Jossey-Bass.

Dumaine, B. (1994). The trouble with teams. *Fortune, 131*(5), 86–92.

Friedman, I. A. (1995). Student behavior patterns contributing to teacher burnout. *Journal of Educational Research*, 88(5), 281–289.

Herman, R. E., & Gioia, J. L. (1998). Making work meaningful: Secrets of the future corporation. *The Futurist, 32*(9), 24–26, 35–38.

Katzenbach, J. R., & Smith, D. K. (1993). *The wisdom of teams*. New York: HarperCollins.

Marshall, E. M. (1995). *Transforming the way we work: The power of collaborative workplace*. Boston: American Management Association.

Odell, S. J., & Ferraro, D. P. (1992). Teacher mentoring and teacher retention. *Journal of Education Teaching, 43*(3), 200–204.

Powers, J. (1996). Cohesive teaching teams—what makes the difference. *Child Care Information Exchange, 109*, 78–81.

Ralston, F. (1995). *Hidden dynamics*. Boston: American Management Association.

Robbins, H., & Finley, M. (1995). *Why teams don't work*. Princeton, NJ: Peterson's/Pacesetter Books.

Turk, R. L. (1994). *Successful procedures for implementing total quality management in UCEA recommended schools*. Unpublished doctoral dissertation, Texas A & M University.

Randall L. Turk is Assistant Professor at Wichita State University, Wichita, KS 67260-0142.

PART IV

PLANNING COMPREHENSIVE TEACHER SUPPORT

Combining Mentoring and Assessment in California

Bob Schultz

California's successful two-year program helps new teachers not only make smooth transitions into the classroom but also choose to stay in the teaching profession.

Statistics predict a need for 0.5 million to 2.5 million new teachers over the next decade. This demand for new teachers is the result of increasing numbers of students, which we can't control; class-size reduction programs, which we applaud; and retirements, which we all face someday. Robert J. Smalley, director of the California Commission on Teacher Credentialing, identified another factor. In the *Sacramento Bee*,[1] Smalley lamented that an estimated 35 percent of new teachers quit within one year.

This figure is of special concern in California, whose teaching force in 1996 made up almost 9 percent of the 2.7 million public school teachers in the United States. Since that time, reduced class sizes in grades K–3 have exacerbated the need for more teachers in California. The rapid growth in the need for teachers that came with class-size reduction only accelerated the problem as districts competed with one another to get qualified, credentialed candidates to join their teaching ranks. Considering the time, effort, and money that go into the preservice training, recruiting, and ongoing staff development for new teachers, Smalley's statement suggests that we are throwing away one dollar out of every three that we spend on training new teachers. This money could be better spent in the classroom, helping students learn.

Beginning Teacher Support and Assessment

California educators recognized this problem more than a decade ago and started the California New Teacher Project, a research program conducted from 1988 to 1992 that examined alternative strategies for supporting and assessing beginning teachers. From that research came the Beginning Teacher Support and Assessment (BTSA) program in 1992. BTSA grew from a few small projects serving fewer than 10 percent of eligible teachers into a statewide program that could potentially serve every eligible first- and second-year teacher in California in 1999–2000.

Beverly K. Young, associate director of teacher education for the California State University system (which produces 60 percent of California's teachers), called BTSA "the most powerful state program that California—or any state—has ever had in teacher education." Echoing Young's sentiments, legislators in California have increased the budget for BTSA from $7 million in 1996–97 to $17 million in 1997–98 to $67 million in 1998–99.

When I asked Margaret Olebe, a former BTSA director who is now with the California Commission on Teacher Credentialing, why the program has received so much support, she replied, "BTSA has been able to demonstrate through local retention studies that it is more cost effective to invest in BTSA—resulting in a 93 percent retention rate—than to spend money on recruiting each year."

One Teacher's Experience

Positive statistics and cost savings are important facets of the program that keep legislators happy, but how does BTSA affect classroom teachers? Gwyn Readinger was hired as a new teacher at a school in the Rio Linda Union School District near Sacramento. The school has a large population of students who speak English as a second language, a high number of students on free or reduced-cost lunch, and a rapid teacher-turnover rate. In her first year, she was 1 of 16 new teachers at the school. To add to her challenge, California's class-size reduction program was in its first year, and the school's lack of facilities meant that Gwyn taught a group of 20 youngsters while sharing a room for most of the day with another beginning teacher and her 20 students. Even with these challenges, Gwyn chose to commit to the two-year BTSA program, something her room partner chose not to do.

The situation didn't get easier as the year progressed, and both teachers struggled to be successful with their students and competent in the eyes of their evaluator. One difference between the two teachers was that Gwyn worked closely with a BTSA support provider and participated in activities that are part of the BTSA program, whereas the other teacher worked with a mentor teacher who was supportive but did not have the training or resources that BTSA offered. By the end of the school year, the second teacher was asked to leave the school. Gwyn, in contrast, was welcomed back, this time to her own classroom.

At the end of her second year, Gwyn described her experience as a new teacher:

> Without the validation and encouragement from my support provider, I doubt that I would have remained in the teaching profession. Now that I have nearly completed my second year, I feel that I have grown so much professionally and have gained more confidence in my teaching. I also feel that I have learned a great deal about myself as a teacher and about my students.
>
> What is most valuable to me is the continual practice of reflection, which has guided me in modifying my teaching practices so that student outcomes more closely match learning goals. For example, I have learned that my at-risk 1st grade students need clearly stated behavioral expectations for each learning activity or procedure and that they have to have these procedures modeled and practiced with supervision.

Success in Sacramento

What is the program and why is it having such a positive impact? BTSA is a collection of consortiums that bring together school districts, county offices, the University of California system, and the California State University system in similar but individually tailored affiliations.

The project directors across the state meet regularly and make decisions about the key elements that all projects must contain. Because basic principles and guidelines unite all programs, one program, the Sacramento BTSA Consortium, can illustrate how BTSA works.

The Sacramento BTSA Consortium began serving teachers during the 1994–95 school year with a consortium of eight school districts and a loose connection to California State University, Sacramento. The consortium has grown from 150 teachers to nearly 500 teachers. It unites 17 districts in three counties with California State University in a strong partnership that addresses teacher needs in the preservice year and in the first two years of teaching.

The Sacramento Consortium—like all BTSA programs—is guided by the California Standards for the Teaching Profession, a set of standards developed by BTSA and adopted by the Commission on Teacher Credentialing in 1997. Beginning teachers learn about the standards through professional development programs offered on Saturdays through the BTSA program, district training sessions, and one-on-one or small-group work with a trained support provider.

Each teacher develops an Individual Induction Plan that delves deeply into one of the state teaching standards, using a professional portfolio to show evidence of progress. The trained support provider meets regularly with the new teacher—two hours a week in the first few months—and conducts both informal and formal observations that he or she shares with the new teacher. Throughout the two-year relationship, the pair focuses on standards, reflects on practice, and takes action on the basis of reflections and information gathered.

Two-Year Partnerships

The next element in the program is possibly the most important: the relationship between the new teacher and the trained support provider. The key factor here is *training*. California has had a mentor teacher program for about 15 years, but before BTSA, it offered no formal statewide training on how to work with new teachers. The funding structure of BTSA allots $3,000 each year for each new teacher, with the districts providing $2,000 in matching funds. This structure has led to a tight bond between the mentor program and BTSA. Most districts have chosen to use their mentors as the support providers for the program.

The mentor or support provider goes through a week of training before even beginning to work with the new teacher and then has ongoing training throughout the year. That training gives a structure and a consistency to the process, which has improved the mentor's ability to systematically help new teachers. A positive side effect is that mentors improve in their own classrooms. As Mary Landy, a mentor from the Sacramento City Unified School District, put it, "I think I have become a better teacher. BTSA puts such an emphasis on self-reflection for the beginning teachers that I have become more reflective, too."

That emphasis on self-reflection is at the heart of the BTSA process. The support providers are trained not to give answers but to help new teachers analyze the evidence, look at the standards, reflect on the results, and come to their own conclusions. The program develops skills that teachers will use long after their support is gone. As beginning teacher Laurette Gaberman described, "I automatically reflect on lessons, evaluate them, and find ways to change them for the better. I have learned to be objective and can even assess what I do with the eyes of an outsider."

Being able to look at one's teaching with the eyes of an outsider results directly from being trained in a formal observation process. Over the years, the Sacramento Consortium has used three instruments for this observation process, and the current model is the California Formative Assessment and Support System for Teachers (CFASST). Although the instruments have changed, the observation has consistently been an extensive process that involves the mentor's collecting information before and during the observation, comparing the results with standards, and sharing the results in great detail with the new teacher. Laura Wong, a beginning teacher from the Elk Grove Unified School District, stated,

> The greatest benefit for me was to be observed by an objective party who was able to tell me the good things that I was doing and the areas where I could improve. My observer affirmed my strengths but also helped me let myself "off the hook" of perfection. I allow myself to be in a learning process—like the children in my class.

Bernard Baruch said, "Failure is a far better teacher than success." The fact that observations are always confidential—between the new teacher and the support provider, not with the teacher's evaluator—encourages teachers to take more risks and learn quickly.

Up to Standards?

What happens to teachers who don't meet the standards of the program and of their principals? Although statistics demonstrate that teachers in the BTSA program are more likely to remain in the profession, some teachers still struggle and don't meet standards. A few of these go on to other districts and find success in a new setting, whereas others realize in their first year that teaching is not for them. Our BTSA program brings them to that realization quickly so they can get a fresh start after only a year, rather than wait until they feel burned out several years down the line. The early realization of a career mistake is a plus for both the redirected teacher and for the students who would have had that teacher and may be one of the most important outcomes of the BTSA process.

One outside observer of the BTSA program is the California Educational Research Cooperative, operating out of the University of California, Riverside. The Research Cooperative, working closely with BTSA, has conducted independent evaluations of the program with extensive surveys. When comparing BTSA-trained teachers with other new teachers, the researchers found a significant increase in time for professional reflection and an increased ability to motivate students.

In addition to evaluations, the Sacramento Consortium has an annual planning meeting involving beginning teachers and support providers from every district. That meeting gives teachers a chance to identify what did and did not work. As a result of this input, BTSA leaders are able to simplify, reorganize the program, and implement many revisions.

From Concerns to Quality

We hope that ongoing reflection and improvement will help dispel the fears of people like Jerry Hayward, a codirector of Policy Analysis for California Education, who recently said, "I'm a little concerned because the increase [in participating teachers] is so great that it may be difficult to sustain the quality of the program." This is a great challenge as BTSA shifts from being a small and voluntary program to being a large program expected for all teachers.

The governor of California, Gray Davis, has added another challenge. He recently recommended that the mentor teacher program be discontinued and converted into a peer review program to help struggling veteran teachers. That legislation passed in March 1999. Thus, school districts need to develop and negotiate new delivery systems for mentor services that cover both the peer review requirement and the support for new teachers through a BTSA model.

Finally, for BTSA to truly become institutionalized, site administrators need to understand and support the program. The Sacramento

Consortium has offered administrator breakfasts and one- and two-day introductory sessions on the principles of BTSA; these sessions have expanded into a weeklong training program that focuses on formative assessment, the California Standards for the Teaching Profession, and a modified version of the observation process. Teachers and administrators will now speak the same language and use the same standards to evaluate good teaching.

In the end, however, the value of BTSA will not be measured by savings in recruitment money or by measures of teacher, administrator, or legislator support for the program. To realize its true value, consider the words of beginning teacher Lisa R. Johnson from the Rocklin Unified School District:

> Through my participation in BTSA, I have been able to challenge my teaching practices and reflect on how an effective environment, thorough lesson planning, and dynamic instructional strategies work together to instill learning—academically, socially, and emotionally.

Even more important, the students will be the beneficiaries of the BTSA program. And their success will be the ultimate assessment of the project.

Note

[1] Engellenner, J. (1998, June 21). Pressure on schools tests state's rookie teachers. *The Sacramento Bee*.

Bob Schultz is Assistant Superintendent for Curriculum Instruction in the Eureka Union School District. He may be reached at 4025 Frontera Dr., Davis, CA 95616-6707 (e-mail: bschultz@eureka-usd.k12.ca.us).

A Support Program with Heart: The Santa Cruz Project

Ellen Moir, Janet Gless, and Wendy Baron

Nothing is more important for student learning than the quality of the classroom teacher. A teacher-induction program that focuses on new-teacher support and classroom practice, while sustaining the idealism of beginning teachers, offers hope for our schools.

Beginning teachers enter our nation's classrooms with passion, idealism, and the commitment to make a difference for their students (Fullan, 1993). Too often, however, they find themselves embarking on their journey isolated from their colleagues and faced with difficult working conditions, inadequate materials, and the most challenging classroom assignments. They are shocked by these harsh realities and by a passionless system that has forgotten its most valuable resource—its teachers.

The quality of the teacher is the single most important factor in improving student achievement (Haycock, 1998). An investment in teacher quality needs to start at the earliest stages of a teacher's career and to continue throughout a professional lifetime (National Commission on Teaching and America's Future, 1996). As U.S. schools hire more than two million new teachers in the next decade, we have the chance to transform the teaching profession by creating induction programs that nurture new teachers while promoting the highest standards of classroom teaching.

To do this, we need to break loose of the traditions that have divided educators and to build comprehensive models of teacher development. Universities, schools, administrators, teachers, bargaining units, and teacher educators must come together to create systems grounded in the principles of effective teacher education and professional development. Investing in teacher quality does not involve only beginning teachers and induction programs. Investing in teacher quality involves establishing systemwide norms and practices of professionalism, career-long learning, and inquiry into practice (Darling-Hammond & McLaughlin, 1995). It involves making a commitment to improving education for America's culturally, ethnically, and linguistically diverse students—and to improving the professional lives of the teachers who serve them.

The Santa Cruz New Teacher Project Integrates Support and Assessment

In the past 11 years, the Santa Cruz New Teacher Project (SCNTP) has supported more than 1,400 K–12 teachers making the difficult transition into the teaching profession. The SCNTP is led by the Teacher Education Program at the University of California, Santa Cruz, in collaboration with the Santa Cruz County Office of Education and 16 school districts in the greater Silicon Valley and Santa Cruz area. Together, across institutional boundaries, stakeholders in the consortium have built and sustained a program that nurtures both the heart and the mind of every first- and second-year teacher. Ultimately, the program works to ensure a highly qualified, committed, and inspired teacher for every child.

Currently serving more than 320 beginning teachers, the SCNTP is part of California's Beginning Teacher Support and Assessment (BTSA) program, a statewide initiative jointly administered by the California Department of Education and the California Commission on Teacher Credentialing. The state funds the program at a rate of $3,000 for each beginning teacher. Local districts then augment this funding according to the number of beginning teachers participating in the program at a rate of $2,100 for each teacher. Both the state and the participating districts see this investment in teacher induction as a cost-effective way to promote teacher quality and to increase teacher retention.

Our project's philosophy is that teaching is complex and that the process of becoming a teacher involves career-long learning. We recognize that new teachers enter the profession at different developmental stages and with different needs. We believe that support should be embedded in classroom practice and suffused with the language of hope, caring, and equity. In addition, we have learned that changes in instruction are most likely to occur when teachers are given the opportunity to assess their practice against recognized professional standards and to construct solutions to their own classroom-specific challenges.

Partnerships Between New and Veteran Teachers

At the center of our work are the partnerships that form between the beginning teachers and the new-teacher advisors, exemplary veteran teachers on loan full-time from participating districts for two to three years. Matched with beginning teachers according to grade level and subject-matter expertise, each advisor mentors 14 first- and second-year teachers.

Building strong, trusting relationships with new teachers is the crucial first step for advisors and is fundamental to the success of their work. Advisors meet weekly with each new teacher for two hours before, during, or after school. While in the classroom, advisors teach demonstration lessons, observe, coach, coteach, videotape lessons, respond to interactive journals, or assist with problems that arise. Familiarity with the students in the class, the overall curriculum plan, and the organizational environment helps advisors provide advisees with context-specific support. Advisors spend time outside the classroom planning, gathering resources, providing emotional support and safe structures for feedback, and communicating with principals.

In addition, new teachers receive release days for observation of other teachers, curriculum planning, reflection, and self-assessment. A monthly seminar series serves as a network in which new teachers can share their accomplishments and challenges with a community of peers (Lieberman, 1995). Seminar participants pay special attention to literacy, language development, and strategies for working with diverse student populations, including English Language Learners.

With their advisors, beginning teachers develop portfolios that document their professional growth while encouraging reflection, goal setting, dialogue, and assessment. This collaborative portfolio process is a central feature of our model of support and assessment, and the process helps beginning teachers connect teaching, learning, and assessment. A second-year teacher and program graduate notes,

> The portfolio process has supported me in many ways. It gave me an understanding of where I was and a vision of where I was going and how to get there. Without some way of focusing during those overwhelming first years of teaching, you can feel as if you are not moving forward. The reflection and documentation helped me see the progress I had actually made.

Key to this portfolio process are the advisor's guidance and assistance, beginning with the collection of information about the new teacher's classroom practice. The new teachers then use these data as they self-assess on the Santa Cruz New Teacher Project's *Developmental Continuum of Teacher Abilities*. The continuum is aligned with the *California Standards for the Teaching Profession* (California Commission on Teacher Credentialing and the California Department of Education, 1997), which are organized around broad categories of knowledge, skills, and abilities that characterize effective teaching: organizing and managing the classroom, planning and delivering instruction, demonstrating subject-matter knowledge, assessing student learning, and participating as members of a learning community.

The continuum is a tool for formative assessment and a catalyst for reflection and professional dialogue. With the help of their advisors, new teachers develop an individual learning plan that is based on information gathered during this assessment and focused on a particular standard.

Over the course of the year, the weekly interactions between the new teacher and the advisor and the monthly seminars support portfolio development. Advisors help new teachers select representative items for their portfolios. These typically include journal entries, documented observations, student work, lesson plans, teacher-created materials and assessments, letters, pictures, videotapes, and audiotapes. A written explanation accompanies each item and describes how the item demonstrates the teacher's professional growth or the growth of the students in relation to professional goals. The portfolio process also helps advisors identify the most effective form of assistance for their mentees.

Considering the Impact on Teachers and Schools

New teachers report that participation in our program has made a significant contribution to the quality of their teaching and to their success as beginning teachers, an observation echoed by their principals. A pilot research study of student literacy development has shown that student achievement in the classrooms of participating new teachers matches that of students taught by veteran teachers. Evaluation studies also show that these beginning teachers exhibit increased job satisfaction, are retained at higher rates, work more effectively with diverse students, and are better able to solve problems around issues of instruction and student achievement. Beginning teachers also report that they welcome the regular observations by their advisors and find them essential for their professional growth.

School officials and administrators also note the positive impact of our program. In a recent survey of principals, 95 percent of respondents credited the Santa Cruz New Teacher Project with significantly improving beginning teacher performance. Principals cited specific outcomes: better new-teacher morale, increased willingness to take risks, more effective problem-solving strategies, improved classroom management and organization, and more effective instructional strategies.

We have also found that the teacher induction program involves not only supporting new teachers; it also involves developing teacher leaders and ultimately changing school cultures. Our alumni are making an impact on school cultures even after they are no longer participating in the SCNTP. Principals note that our collaborative model of support is changing the relationships among teachers and promoting the establishment of professional norms for entire staffs.

SCNTP alumni have learned to welcome the opportunities to observe and to be observed by their colleagues; their doors are always open. They are assuming leadership roles early in their careers as they make on-site presentations to colleagues, attend literacy study groups, encourage veteran colleagues to try new strategies, engage in collaborative action research, and request sanctioned time to observe and coach one another. As a result, administrators are beginning to set aside time at staff meetings to allow reflective conversations and problem solving on a monthly basis; others are finding ways to enable colleagues to observe one another in the classroom.

In addition, our veteran advisors return to their school districts with renewed excitement and passion for teaching, a broader perspective on education, and the communication and leadership skills to make a difference. After working in numerous schools and visiting many classrooms in the company of their advisees, our advisors develop a wonderfully rich picture of education across our region. After 15 or more years of teaching, these veterans have stepped out of the unique circumstances of their own classroom practice into a more expansive professional landscape.

They also return to their classrooms with new ideas and fresh approaches. An advisor notes,

> In working with [my colleagues] in a reflective manner, I am becoming more reflective about my own practice and its effects on students. And through our work to implement various strategies, my own repertoire of teaching methods is ever increasing. When I return to a classroom of students, I will bring with me an enriched and stronger practice.

Returning advisors also note that they will never go back to the way things were before. They return to their classrooms with a renewed commitment to and passion for teaching. They have learned to see themselves—and their new teachers—as change agents who have the capacity to change schools by providing strong educational and instructional leadership.

These former advisors serve as school-site and districtwide curriculum leaders, union representatives, professional development school coordinators, and site administrators. One has successfully led the reform of her district's teacher-evaluation process, shifting it to a collaborative model of focused professional growth that uses the SCNTP *Continuum of Teacher Abilities*.

Lessons Learned: What Makes the Difference

As beginning teachers analyze and share their growth over time, the program coordinators continually seek to identify lessons about new-teacher support and assessment. We feel that our success rests in important fundamental features of our model and in our project's commitment to nurture the hearts as well as the minds of our participants—both the veteran and the beginner.

Some of the most significant insights include (1) the importance of the veteran teacher as a full-time advisor, (2) the crucial link to site administration, and (3) the impact of standards embedded within a compassionate, supportive environment.

A New Role for Veteran Teachers

After 11 years of using a full-time release model of advising, we are convinced that this design feature is key to the success of the Santa Cruz New Teacher Project. It is the quality of the relationship that these talented veterans forge with each new teacher and their day-to-day guidance that ultimately have an impact on the quality of a new teacher's instruction.

We have found that supporting new teachers is complex and demanding work and that it involves learning skills other than those that most classroom teachers possess. Providing this support becomes even harder when advisors must simultaneously focus on the needs of students in their own classrooms. Supporting new teachers after the school day ends makes it difficult to understand a new teacher's classroom circumstances, his or her level of practice, and the students' needs.

With a full-time release model, our advisors are able to observe beginning teachers weekly, sometimes collecting formal observation data, other times assisting with or coteaching a lesson. The advisor and the advisee become a classroom team in which the energy is fully focused on the beginning teacher's needs. We are also able to ensure that our veteran teachers' time is totally sanctioned for the work of one-on-one advising. For three years, they are not available to pick up other duties or to split their focus by supporting other initiatives.

Further, supporting 14 beginning teachers every day for an entire school year builds mentoring skills quickly; our advisors become skilled coaches, classroom observers, and group facilitators almost overnight. At the same time, important differences exist between our first- and third-year advisors. In many ways, first-year advisors are like beginning teachers, learning the procedures and processes that characterize their new role; they are learning to examine and deconstruct their knowledge of teaching. Third-year advisors become important contributors to the development and refinement of our program.

As we select advisors each year, we remember what we learned early on—that not every outstanding veteran teacher makes an effective advisor. Thus, we pay close attention to the following criteria: strong interpersonal skills, credibility with peers and administrators, a demonstrated curiosity and eagerness to learn, respect for multiple perspectives, and outstanding instructional practice. We know that strong advisors can easily develop observation and coaching skills, knowledge of California's professional standards, familiarity with the portfolio process, support strategies for new teachers, and group facilitation and presentation skills.

Regardless of how carefully we select our advisors, however, high-quality support doesn't just happen. Providing thoughtful assistance to beginning teachers requires training and support for the advisors. Advisors receive a half-day orientation to the program and two days of foundational training, followed by weekly staff development. Friday morning staff meetings have become a cherished ritual and an important component of our program's success. Not only do the meetings prepare advisors for their work, but also they break down the potential isolation that many full-time advisors experience as they travel from school to school, supporting their advisees.

We use this time to review project procedures and our assessment tools and their use. We practice observation skills by using videotaped lessons of beginning teachers. We review and develop our advisors' familiarity with the *California Standards for the Teaching Profession* not just as a lens on good teaching, but as a way to keep all eyes focused on improving classroom practice. Together we read articles, share concerns, practice facilitation and presentation skills, and, most important, think about and talk about our work. The meetings also give us important feedback on our program's implementation and effectiveness.

Strong Links to Site Administrators

Principals have always been an important part of the Santa Cruz New Teacher Project's stakeholder loop, but with each successive year, we become more convinced of the crucial role that administrators must play in the web of support we want to build. Their understanding of new teachers' needs affects how they design classroom assignments, and the site culture has a significant impact on our new teachers' lives. Further, their commitment to and support of our work is crucial are our advisors' success.

As a result, we seek to make site administrators our partners in our work. Advisors check in with administrators on a regular basis to update them on the work that is being done with new teachers, while maintaining strict lines of confidentiality. They may point out that the new teachers are being videotaped or formally observed, are self-assessing by using the SCNTP continuum, are attending an after-school seminar on student assessment, are observing a veteran teacher's class, or are developing their professional growth goals for the year.

The administrator's support of our program can also influence the beginning teacher's own commitment to the process of professional reflection, assessment, ongoing learning, and collaboration. In addition, the SCNTP can become an important collaborative partner in principals' efforts to develop their staff and to meet site instructional goals. Sometimes the number of new teachers is so large that an advisor is stationed full-time at a given school site, thus having even greater influence on schoolwide instructional improvement and cultural change.

Addressing Standards with Heart

High professional standards are essential for all educators, and the role of any induction program must be to help new teachers recognize the standards and put them into practice. But in these times of standards-based curriculums and standards-driven reform, we feel that standards alone do not ensure quality teaching. However, when standards are embedded in a compassionate and responsive system of support, they can guide educational reform.

Instructional change is developmental, is individual, and rests in the hands of each and every classroom teacher. We have noticed over the years that virtually all new teachers walk into classrooms seeing themselves as agents for change, not as defenders of the status quo. We further believe that the highest standards of practice will be achieved when the passion and the inspiration that accompany most new teachers into the profession are carefully celebrated and nurtured. In the SCNTP, we have found that when new teachers are in the company of veteran teachers who embody the highest standards of practice and who still radiate a passion for teaching, new teachers not only thrive, but also meet high standards and live out the promise of change that called them to become teachers in the first place.

In our program, we have learned to speak the language of the heart, to remind teachers of why they chose to enter the profession, to celebrate our own learning as well as that of our students, to remind ourselves that equity and excellence must go hand in hand, to articulate the connections between what we believe and how we act in the world, and to practice our art and craft with congruence. Speaking the language of the heart is perhaps the most important gift we give new teachers. No carefully designed system of support, no technology or structure, no assessment system or standards can replace the heartfelt commitment to education and to students that drives the finest of our teachers.

So we have embedded the *California Standards for the Teaching Profession* in every aspect of our program—in our seminars, our assessments, our collaborative log forms, and, most important, in our language. And at the same time, we seek to create compassionate environments for new teachers in which they hear the language of inspiration and love, of passion for teaching and dedication to community, of commitment to excellence and a determination that every child be afforded the birthright of a quality education. Our children and our schools deserve no less.

References

California Commission on Teacher Credentialing and the California Department of Education. (1997). *California standards for the teaching profession*. Sacramento, CA: Author.

Darling-Hammond, L., & McLaughlin, M. W. (1995, April). Policies that support professional development in an era of reform. *Phi Delta Kappan,76*(8), 597–604.

Fullan, M. (1993, March). Why teachers must become change agents. *Educational Leadership*, 50(6), 12–17.

Haycock, K. (1998, Summer). Good teaching matters: How well-qualified teachers can close the gap. *Thinking K–16*, 3(2), 1–2.

Lieberman, A. (1995, April). Practices that support teacher development: Transforming conceptions of professional learning. *Phi Delta Kappan*, 76(8), 591–596.

National Commission on Teaching and America's Future. (1996). *What matters most: Teaching for America's future*. Kutztown, PA: Kutztown Publishing.

Ellen Moir is Director, **Janet Gless** is Associate Director, and **Wendy Baron** is Associate Director of the New Teacher Center at the University of California, Santa Cruz, 809 Bay Ave., Capitola, CA 95010.

How Can New Teachers Become the BEST?

Ann L. Wood

Saturday seminars spell success in California, where mentor teachers support novices in their quest to develop professionally. The state's professional teaching standards are the framework for the Beginning Educators' Seminars on Teaching (BEST).

Sherie, 40, is a first-year elementary school teacher for whom teaching was the fulfillment of a lifelong dream. When Sherie was an intern, her site principal noticed her strong teaching abilities, outgoing personality, and unusual dedication. He took a personal interest in her teaching career, offered her advice during her internship, and encouraged her to stay at his school site during her first official year of teaching.

As the teacher of a 1st and 2nd grade combination class with students from many language backgrounds, Sherie worked diligently at maintaining each learner's ethnic integrity. In Saturday seminars, she participated in learning activities based on the *California Standards for the Teaching Profession* (CSTP) (California Commission on Teacher Credentialing and the California Department of Education, 1997). Sherie used the standards to assess her own teaching, and she developed a classroom-research question to foster her professional growth: "How can I develop teaching strategies that address different student learning styles?" Over the year, she compiled student work and evidence of her teaching practices into a teaching portfolio (WestEd, 1997).

During her first year of teaching, Sherie had two mentors—her principal and her mentor in the Beginning Educators' Seminars on Teaching (BEST) program. Each held regular conversations with her, observed her teaching, listened to her concerns, and offered advice when she asked for it. They provided different perspectives, two backdrops from which she could view teaching as her chosen profession. Latisha, her BEST mentor, conducted four formal, standards-based observations of Sherie's teaching as it related to her research question. She offered Sherie emotional support and suggestions for classroom management, curriculum planning, assessment, and educational materials. Latisha helped Sherie understand how to meet state and district curriculum standards while individualizing instruction for her culturally diverse students. She reinforced the BEST seminars' emphasis on the importance of reflective conversations and writing. Sherie completed her first year of teaching with a deeper understanding of school and a greater trust in administration than are usually present in novice teachers.

Induction That Works

Researchers have identified four components in successful teacher induction programs: (1) teaching standards, (2) mentoring, (3) reflective teaching practices, and (4) some type of *formative* assessment system (Gray & Gray, 1985). (Formative assessment is a system in which the work of a teacher is collected over time and measured against set criteria for best teaching practices. The purpose of formative assessment, which is a summative evaluation, is to promote an individual teacher's reflections on his or her ongoing professional growth.) Together these four components form the basis for the Beginning Educators' Seminars on Teaching (BEST).

The Beginning Educators' Seminars on Teaching is based on California's new state-sponsored teacher induction program, the Beginning Teacher Support and Assessment (BTSA) program. BEST is a series of professional development seminars held on Saturdays for beginning inner-city teachers that incorporates these four components. At the seminars, teachers gain concrete insights into the *California Standards for the Teaching Profession* (California Commission on Teacher Credentialing and the California Department of Education, 1997) and the California Teaching Portfolio (CTP) model (WestEd, 1997). BEST seminars are conducted on 16 Saturday mornings during the school year to avoid the overextension of time that novice teachers experience in mandated after-school commitments on Mondays through Thursdays.

BEST is a collaborative program between the San Diego City Schools and San Diego State University. BEST offers seminars for K–12 teachers that are designed around each of the six California standards. The seminars provide regular forums for concentrated, collegial peer interactions in small-group settings.

For example, during the BEST seminars, novice teachers complete an educational materials budget simulation in which they select and order appropriate educational resources. Seminar participants experiment with various cooperative learning group activities and behavior management techniques. They critique one another's school to home communications and lesson plans. And novice teachers map out their communities and identify resources to support their students' individualized needs.

Teaching Standards Are the Foundation

Adopted in 1997, the California Standards for the Teaching Profession encompass six teaching standards: (1) engaging and supporting all students in learning, (2) creating and maintaining effective environments for student learning, (3) understanding and organizing subject matter for student learning, (4) planning instruction and designing learning experiences for all students, (5) assessing student learning, and (6) developing as a professional educator (California Commission on Teacher Credentialing and the California Department of Education, 1997).

The standards form the foundation on which California's state-supported teacher induction program, the Beginning Teacher Support and Assessment (BTSA), is based. The standards also ground the new California Formative Assessment and Support System for Teachers (CFASST). The system identifies the developmental levels of teaching practices for key elements of each of the six standards in its Descriptions of Practice. Collaborating with support providers, novice teachers use the Descriptions of Practice to self-assess their teaching.

Selecting the Right Mentors

In the California program, new-teacher mentors are anchors for beginning teachers. They provide a safety net in troubling times and guide each beginning teacher on the journey from neophyte to mature teacher. Mentors make just enough waves to push new teachers gently forward in their practice.

The success of establishing a system of peer mentors for new teachers lies in the selection and matching processes. For mentoring to be effective, program coordinators must select mentors on the basis of their interest in forming relationships with new teachers, not on seniority. Mentors need to be dedicated to coaching new teachers in flexible, nondirective ways; they should not view their mentoring positions as entitlements for years served. Similarly, after the mentor selection process, program coordinators must match mentors with new teachers on the basis of school site; grade-level experience; curriculum content; and specialization, such as bilingual education or special education.

Each novice teacher in the BEST program is assigned a mentor teacher with more than four years of experience in the school district. BEST mentors have informal on-site contacts with the new teachers and are expected to conduct four, standards-based, formal observations throughout the school year. These observations are followed by collaborative reflective conversations and written reflections on the teaching activities and on how well students learned. New teachers write reflections on plans to adjust their teaching techniques or behavioral management strategies to techniques that better match students' needs.

One novice teacher, Stephen, 42, is a former military professional. He is trilingual and has traveled around the world. His cultural exposure and language proficiency made him particularly empathetic to the wide cultural and linguistic diversity of his 3rd grade class. Thirty-five percent of the students spoke Spanish, 10 percent spoke Vietnamese, and 5 percent spoke Tagalog. Ten percent of the students were African American, and 40 percent were European American. During the school year, he taught his 3rd graders basic phrases in several languages.

Although Stephen seemed particularly suited for this class of 3rd graders, his BEST mentor, Alice, discovered that Stephen was experiencing typical first-year struggles with student behavioral management. Regardless of his prior professional experiences, Stephen was still a new teacher establishing control in his lively classroom.

Stephen and Alice talked at length throughout his first year. She provided him with professional tips, encouragement, and support that helped him better manage his classroom. She was the human bridge from the teaching standards discussed in the BEST seminars to the practice he was creating during his first year of teaching. She listened patiently, challenged him to think about issues, and was a presence in his professional life. They became close colleagues and established a professional relationship that went well beyond his first year of teaching.

Reflective Teaching Practices

Paulo Freire (1970) demonstrated the power of teaching that is based on action and reflection—a combination he called "praxis." Freire's integration of reflection and action became the foundation for one of the world's most successful literacy programs. The potency of his ideas can be transmitted to new teachers. Beginning educators can learn to become reflective practitioners.

The BEST program advocates the cycle of planning, teaching, reflecting, and applying. The program encourages novice teachers to carefully plan each teaching strategy or behavioral management approach that they implement. As they teach a particular lesson or use an individual behavioral management technique, they reflect on what and how students learned. Novices write reflections for their teaching portfolios about teaching episodes and artifacts. After reflection, the program encourages teachers to adapt the lesson, strategy, or technique and to take action. Each new application or adaptation of a lesson then leads to more planning, teaching, and reflecting. The cycle spirals on and on.

The BEST seminar series develops reflective teaching skills through conversations and writings about teaching. Each seminar includes time for novice teachers to examine issues and concerns related to their individual teaching assignments. Participants discuss aspects of reflective conversation. New teachers practice reflective listening and nonjudgmental conversational techniques. As they practice these reflective conversation skills with their peers, they became more self-accepting of their own teaching abilities.

BEST seminar participants complete written reflections on each seminar activity and assignment. At each seminar, the program coordinator gives new teachers reflective stems to trigger their thoughts about teaching practices and to encourage them to write their ideas and feelings about teaching. Examples of these reflective stems follow:

- This observation showed me that this group of students is . . .
- From using this strategy, what I learned about the students' learning is . . .
- This material is culturally relevant to the students in my class because . . .

Formative Assessment Systems Form Effective Professionals

Fifty percent of California's teachers were leaving the profession in the first five years of teaching. Research shows that for school districts that operate BTSA programs, however, the overall teacher attrition rate has dropped to less than 10 percent (California Commission on Teacher Credentialing and the California Department of Education, 1992).

Not all states have an established formative assessment system. Analyzing new-teacher systems that do exist can help others make appropriate adaptations of their own. Education leaders can find models in the California Formative Assessment and Support System for Teachers (CFASST), Pathwise, and the WestEd portfolio. CFASST is an integrated formative assessment and support system developed by the California Commission on Teacher Credentialing, the California Department of Education, and the Educational Testing Service as the basis for BTSA programs (Danielson, 1996). Pathwise is a teacher induction program developed by Educational Testing Service. The program trains mentors to support novice teachers by using four domains of professional responsibility within a framework for teaching.

The WestEd California Teaching Portfolio (CTP) forms the groundwork for BEST. The CTP model is a teaching portfolio in which novice teachers collect evidence that their teaching practices reflect key elements of the California Standards for the Teaching Profession. Further, each BEST seminar participant identifies one central question about his or her professional growth. This becomes a classroom-based research question and the focal point for the teaching portfolio. Throughout the year, each teacher collects artifacts or evidence of his or her teaching practices based on this question.

Tanya's classroom-based research question was, "How can I use literacy portfolios to increase my 2nd graders' active participation in the writing process?" Through exploring this classroom-based research question, Tanya was able to implement her school's mandatory student literacy portfolios while she learned about BEST teaching portfolios.

Tom posed a different research question: "How can I connect students' life experiences and interests with 8th grade science curriculum objectives and learning goals?" Throughout his first year of teaching, Tom instituted learning activities that reflected his students' linguistic and cultural backgrounds. Rich colors, sights, and sounds abounded in his classroom, which was filled to the brim with displays of student work. Tom commented that focusing on his classroom-based research question helped him "accomplish his goals and think more about his teaching."

Professional Discourse That Leads to Results

Barth (1990) suggests that creating opportunities for professional discourse leads to greater experimentation among teachers. The BEST teachers' research resulted in their increased experimentation with new teaching techniques and curricular lessons. Being a part of a formative assessment system encouraged them to view teaching as developmental and dynamic. They began to view themselves as lifelong learners. One participant said, "I'm using the lessons that were successful and trying new techniques shared by the BEST speakers." Another noted, "I seek out help from references, resources, other teachers, and other classrooms to meet the needs of individual students, not just the majority."

By participating in a formative assessment and support program that is valid and reliable, new teachers learn about teaching standards, reflection, and self-assessment of their teaching practices. Mentors provide beginning teachers with models for internalizing their role as educators. The teacher induction program provides new teachers with peer support for experimentation with different teaching techniques for which they are developmentally ready. As new teachers grow professionally through the reflection and action cycle, they are able to link ideas and practices for their own definition of the BEST teaching.

References

Barth, R. (1990). *Improving schools from within.* San Francisco: Jossey-Bass.

California Commission on Teacher Credentialing and the California Department of Education. (1992). *Success for beginning teachers: Final report of the California new teacher project.* Sacramento, CA: Author.

California Commission on Teacher Credentialing and the California Department of Education. (1997). *California standards for the teaching profession.* Sacramento, CA: Author.

Danielson, C. (1996). *Enhancing professional practice: A framework for teaching.* Alexandria, VA: ASCD.

Freire, P. (1970). *Pedagogy of the oppressed.* New York: Seabury Press.

Gray, W. A., & Gray, M. M. (1985, November). Synthesis of research on mentoring beginning teachers. *Educational Leadership*, *43*, 37–43.

WestEd. (1997). *A guide to preparing beginning teachers and support providers to work with the California teaching portfolio.* San Francisco: Author.

Ann L. Wood is Lecturer for the College of Education, San Diego State University, San Diego, CA 92182-1153 (e-mail: alwood@mail.sdsu.edu).

Developing a Common Language and Spirit

John G. Conyers, Bob Ewy, and Linda Vass

A mandatory four-year teacher induction-mentoring program gives new teachers the support and encouragement they need to succeed and excel.

If you've been in a classroom on the opening day of school, as we often have, you know the look—it's a combination of excitement and terror! No, not the students—the teachers. Those assured, confident graduates who were thrilled with their new teaching jobs and could hardly wait until school started now have absolute panic on their faces. They have suddenly realized the huge responsibility they have undertaken, and they're scared.

For most new teachers, the first few months—even years—are a roller coaster of joyful exhilaration and abject fear. Fortunately, the majority of new teachers quickly learn to cope and become successful teachers, but their attrition rate is high, which leads to enormous costs both in human terms and in dollars expended. And as school districts continue to raise the bar on performance as they move teaching to an even more professional level, the pressure on new teachers and the risk of failure increase.

Community Consolidated School District 15 in Palatine, Illinois, employs more than 900 certified staff in 19 schools: 14 K–6 schools, 3 junior high schools, 1 K–8 school, and 1 special education school. District 15, with 12,620 students, is the second-largest elementary school district in Illinois. Seventy-two percent of the students are white and non-Hispanic and 16 percent are Hispanic. More than 60 languages are spoken in the homes of our students.

Every year, more than 90 of the district's teachers are new, either to teaching or to the district. We're fortunate to have about 2,500 applicants for teaching positions each year. They come from all over the country, bringing varying levels of experience and talent. Our rigorous selection process, carefully designed to identify candidates who meet our high expectations, includes careful screening of the initial paperwork, a telephone interview, technology and literacy screening, extensive principal involvement, peer interviews, and a requirement for writing samples. Still, despite our best hiring efforts, we've historically had a relatively high new-teacher attrition rate.

This concern impelled District 15 to look for a consistent way of offering our new teachers the assistance that would enable them not only to survive those first critical days and years, but also to grow and to develop into the excellent teachers that our community demands and deserves. We believe that new employees are key to our goal of supporting a culture of excellence.

As the National Commission on Teaching and America's Future (1996) notes,

> Ultimately, the quality of teaching depends not only on the qualifications of individuals hired, but also on how schools structure teaching work and teachers' learning opportunities. (p. 82)

Designing an Induction-Mentoring Program

As we explored the best methods of providing structured support for our new teachers, we quickly recognized that a formal induction program with a strong mentoring component was the best avenue to achieve our objectives. The professional literature supports this conclusion:

> It is important to clarify that . . . for a beginning-teacher program to be considered an induction program it must contain some degree of systematic and sustained assistance and not merely be a series of orientation meetings or a formal evaluation process used for teachers new to the profession. (Huling-Austin, 1990, p. 48)

Research demonstrates that successful teacher induction programs have coordinators, well-trained mentors, and flexible structures to meet the needs of new teachers over time (Dagenais, 1996; Huling-Austin, 1992; Huling-Austin, Odell, Ishler, Kay, & Edelfdelt, 1989). District 15's program has been carefully structured to incorporate all those elements.

The Evolution of the Program

The "Helping Teacher" induction program began in 1987 as part of the district's collective bargaining agreement. Teachers new to the district participated in an induction-mentoring program as a condition of employment.

We started our program with two days of training before school opened. We had no formal curriculum because of a lack of time, but we tried to give new teachers an overview of the district and classroom management strategies. Feedback from participants quickly demonstrated several things: We needed more time and a more structured relationship between new teachers and their mentors, and our mentors needed specific training because some weren't sure what we expected of them.

Since that initial effort, District 15's induction-mentoring program has expanded to include both pre-opening-day sessions and other training during the school year. We first moved to five days. This year it's an eight-day program, on the way to a planned ten days by the year 2001. We strongly support release time for program participants, but feedback has shown that our teachers don't want to be out of their classrooms. With this understanding, we're considering the possibility of Saturday sessions.

We now have a full-time teacher induction facilitator-trainer who has National Board of Professional Teaching Standards certification. She has the major responsibility for coordinating our induction-mentoring program. The facilitator worked closely with the district's personnel department to develop a four-year curriculum, which corresponds to the district's four-year probationary period.

The District 15 Induction Program Goals

Our comprehensive four-year induction curriculum for teachers who are new to Community Consolidated School District 15, whether novice teachers or teachers entering the district, is based on the mentoring program standards from the Mentoring and Leadership Resource Network of the Association for Supervision and Curriculum Development. The curriculum has six specific goals:

- *To improve teaching performance.* All aspects of teaching performance, including classroom environment, instruction, planning and preparation, and professional responsibilities, are addressed.
- *To establish a collaborative professional team responsible for providing assistance and support for inductees.* This part of the curriculum encom-

passes training for mentors and administrators and familiarizes them with the extensive resources that the district offers to support its teachers.

- *To satisfy state-mandated requirements related to induction and certification.* District 15 is committed to providing an induction program that meets or exceeds Illinois standards.
- *To transmit the culture of the district to teachers new to the system.* New teachers become familiar with the District 15 strategic plan, district and building rules and procedures, employee benefits, district and community facilities, and instructional culture.
- *To increase the retention of promising new members of the teaching staff during the induction years.* District 15 offers support and training to new staff members during the entire induction period.
- *To prepare teachers to become candidates for National Board of Professional Teaching Standards certification.* We hope—but do not require—that at the end of our induction curriculum, participants will be well prepared for certification.

The Induction Curriculum

District 15's program incorporates separate tracks for beginning teachers and experienced teachers who are new to the district. For all participants, the first year of the induction experience includes four days of training before school opens and four half-day release-time opportunities during the school year for meetings with trainers or mentors. At least two classroom observations and three after-school meetings also occur.

In this first year, new teachers focus on the following areas:

- A needs assessment in which identified areas of concern are addressed
- An introduction to District 15 Learner Statements
- Techniques for classroom management, which include creating a classroom atmosphere of respect and rapport, managing classroom procedures, maintaining accurate records, and managing student behavior
- Information on communicating with parents, including conducting parent conferences, reporting student progress, and engaging families in the instructional program

- Information on communicating with students, including using clear and accurate oral and written language
- Instruction in basic self-reflection in teaching, including reflecting precisely and using insights in future teaching
- Observation tips, including observing other teachers and using videotaping for self-evaluation
- Information on how to establish a culture for learning, including the importance of the content, student pride in work, and expectations for learning and achievement
- Instruction in giving quality feedback that is timely, accurate, substantive, constructive, and specific

The agenda for experienced teachers new to District 15 contains many of the same items; additional topics include the following:

- Questioning and discussion techniques, including the quality of questions, student participation, presentation of content, activities and assignments, flexible grouping, structure and pacing, and materials and resources
- Information on assessment and student learning, including congruence with instructional goals, criteria and standards, and use for future planning
- Techniques for engaged learning, including the philosophy of constructivism and engaged learning principles
- An introduction to quality tools, including *Future Force: A Teacher's Handbook for Using TQM in the Classroom* (McClanahan & Wicks, 1993)

Years two and three continue in a similar fashion. Novice teachers work with the following topics: self-reflection as a tool for learning, integrated technology across the curriculum, questioning and discussion techniques, assessment and student learning, engaged learning, quality tools, differentiated instruction, Teacher Expectations Student Achievement (TESA) training and support, portfolio development for self-assessment, action research, and professionalism. Experienced teachers focus on self-reflection as a tool for learning, integrated technology across the curriculum,

TESA training and support, differentiated instruction, portfolio development for self-assessment, action research, and professionalism.

All fourth-year inductees participate in a yearlong course, taught by District 15 National Board for Professional Teaching Standards's–certified teachers, in which they complete a teaching portfolio in their area of expertise. We design the curriculum so that at the end of the four years, our new teachers will be well prepared if they choose to seek certification by the National Board of Professional Teaching Standards. We do not require new teachers to apply for certification, but we sincerely hope that they'll take the initiative on their own.

The Mentoring Curriculum

With a carefully structured curriculum in place for new teachers, we took a hard look at how we might best support our mentor teachers, who are recommended by principals. We increased the stipend for mentor teachers and prepared a comprehensive mentor handbook that contains resources and strategies for providing sustained support for new teachers. The handbook contains background on the role of the mentor and offers practical advice on initiating and sustaining a relationship with the new teacher. Also included are guidelines for becoming a successful mentor—complete with a month-by-month checklist of suggested activities and ideas.

We also designed a two-year mentor-training curriculum. In the first year, mentors focus on the following topics:

- A needs assessment
- Goals of the mentoring process
- The observation process
- Ways to establish rapport and trust
- Time-management issues
- Mentoring processes and relationships, including active listening and feedback
- Self-reflection
- The joys of teaching and learning

In the second year, mentors add the following topics for study:

- Refocusing on the goals of the induction program
- Refining observation skills
- Choosing a coaching model that fits
- Collaborating with other mentors to enrich the process

We have formed a Teacher Induction Advisory Committee to provide additional direction as well as to evaluate feedback from new teachers and mentors. We will continue to use this feedback to enhance and refine both the new-teacher and the mentor facets of our work-in-progress program.

Results of the Program

We know from their responses that our new teachers appreciate the support that the district demonstrates through the induction-mentoring program. They tell us it is more valuable and more extensive than induction programs they've experienced in other districts, and it enables them to understand what the district expects of them and gives them a resource (their mentor) to help address everything from serious professional problems to first-year jitters. Among recent comments were these:

> I was impressed by the enthusiasm with which we were welcomed and the constant emphasis on teacher support. I don't feel alone!
>
> I feel supported and encouraged. I get reassurance that the frustration I feel is not just my own.
>
> I feel as if I'm not alone. The climate lets me feel comfortable with not knowing what to do, as long as I ask.
>
> There is always someone who I know I can go to for help in a nonthreatening way, where I can always ask any questions I have.

We also know that our mentor teachers take their responsibilities seriously. They find serving as a mentor a valuable professional experience that allows them to experience a personal sense of renewal in their own professional careers and to give something back to the teaching profession. Their greatest concern is one of time: balancing their mentoring responsibilities with their regular teaching duties. Of 72 mentor teachers who wrote comments after last fall's workshop, 33 expressed concerns about time:

> Time . . . I find it difficult to manage my own time and to give another teacher time, too. They need the most help at the busiest times of the year.
>
> Giving the amount of time it takes to do all the things we learned . . . time to really care, help, and listen.
>
> My greatest concern is allowing the right amount of time to devote on a constant basis for fulfilling the needs of the new teacher.

When we began our induction-mentoring program, we expected it to reduce our new-teacher attrition. However, we've found that over the past several years, our total attrition rate has remained fairly constant. We attribute this to the fact that a comprehensive induction-mentoring program such as ours actually makes marginal teachers realize more quickly that District 15 is not the place for them. That kind of self-selection helps us maintain our standard of excellence. Nevertheless, beginning with the 1999–2000 school year, we plan to compare inductee turnover rates from year to year to determine whether this program can actually influence our attrition.

Another positive result of our program is the clear indication that our beginning teachers are moving more rapidly through the stages of teacher learning: from novice (survival and discovery) to advanced beginner (experimentation and consolidation), on to competent (mastery and stabilization), proficient (analysis and deliberation), and expert (fluidity and flexibility) (National Evaluation Systems, 1997).

Our district remains strongly committed to providing the best possible induction-mentoring program for our new teachers. Choosing and retaining the most skillful, dedicated teachers is vital to maintaining our culture of excellence. It's an important component of our district's accountability to the community, as well as a responsibility we have to the teaching profession.

References

Dagenais, R. J. (1996, December). Mentoring program standards. *Newsletter of the Mentoring and Leadership Resource Network of ASCD*.

Huling-Austin, L. (1990). Teacher induction programs and internships. In W. Houston, M. Haberman, & J. Sikula (Eds.), *Handbook of research on teacher education*. New York: Macmillan.

Huling-Austin, L. (1992, May/June). Research on learning to teach: Implications for teacher induction and mentoring programs. *Journal of Teacher Education*, *43*(3), 173–180.

Huling-Austin, L., Odell, S.J., Ishler, P., Kay, R.S., & Edelfdelt, R. (1989). *Assisting the beginning teacher*. Reston, VA: Association of Teacher Educators.

McClanahan, E., & Wicks, C. (1993). *Future force: A teacher's handbook for using TQM in the classroom*. Chino Hills, CA: PACT Publishing.

National Commission on Teaching and America's Future. (1996).*What matters most: Teaching for America's future*. New York: Author.

National Evaluation Systems. (1997). *The induction years: The beginning teacher*. Amherst, MA: Author.

John G. Conyers (e-mail: conyersj@esc.ccsd15.K12.il.us) is Superintendent of Schools, **Bob Ewy** is Director of Planning, Staff Development, and Quality Programming and **Linda Vass** is Assistant Superintendent for Personnel and Human Services for Community Consolidated School District 15, Joseph M. Kiszka Educational Service Center, 580 North First Bank Dr., Palatine, IL 60067-8108.

Every Classroom, Every Day: A Professional Development Plan

Barbara Moore

During a 30-year career, a teacher will touch the lives of thousands of students. This yearlong orientation program gives all teachers a strong foundation of classroom competence on which to build their professional lives.

On the overhead projector's screen beamed large numerals: 2026. In one of a series of district administrative meetings in 1996 that focused on improving teaching and learning in the Parkway School District in St. Louis County, Missouri, the superintendent pointed to the number after a few welcoming remarks. His charge to us: "Determine why the number 2026 is important to our district."

The group seated around me speculated broadly. "Is it the number of new kindergarten students?" "The number of substitutes used last year?" "An estimated average increase to teachers' salaries?" "The number of staff?" We were completely off base in our guesses. Then one small group announced, "2026—why, that's the year that beginning teachers hired this year will most likely begin retiring from our district if they become career teachers." Right answer!

As the entire group speculated about the years leading to 2026, one absolute emerged: Because a teacher touches many students during a 30-year career, that teacher's success in the classroom is vital to student success. Each teacher will affect hundreds, if not thousands, of students during that time, influencing their academic achievement, their joy of learning, and their sense of belonging. Giving our beginning teachers the best possible introduction to their careers and providing the support and resources necessary for their growth, regardless of their length of service with the district, could only benefit our students and district.

Prior to 1996, the district offered a brief introduction to Parkway, and each of the district's 28 schools determined the extent of assistance given to teachers new to the profession. These past efforts varied in quality and results. As the Parkway School District embraced the mission of ensuring quality teachers in every classroom, our administrators, staff developers, and curriculum coordinators joined in a comprehensive effort to improve the district's induction program. Drawing on the expertise and skills of many employees, Parkway developed and refined the following plan after a two-year concerted effort to build a strong foundation for our newest colleagues.

Providing an Essential Component: Hiring Well

Because the best way to promote effective teaching and learning is to hire talented, committed individuals, Parkway initially focused on aligning its hiring practices with high standards of professional performance. A structured interview procedure, accompanied by a uniform, multistage interview process, supplied a consistent approach to hiring skilled teachers. Through attention to such essentials as an improved background and recommendation review system and a revised application process and time line, the district achieved greater control over the quality of new employees. Without capable educators, any induction program, regardless of its extent and content, will be inadequate.

Building a Strong Professional Career: A Focus on Classroom Competence

Professional development should be responsive to professionals who are in various stages of their careers but who, at every stage, focus on classroom competence. Every professional development opportunity at Parkway addresses one or more of the district's standards for classroom competence: teaching and learning for every student; content, instruction, and assessment; and professional reflection and professional relationships.

A differentiated delivery of staff development programs exists for teachers from recruitment to retirement; one size does not fit all when meeting the professional growth needs of career educators. Often called Parkway's "Zero to Thirty-Plus Professional Development Plan" to indicate the years from preservice to retirement, the plan focuses all staff development programs on stages of teacher development.

The district's staff development department challenges Parkway's tenured veterans to pursue areas of intensive study or to initiate in-depth research on topics of content, instruction, and assessment. This department also coordinates the entry-level stage of professional development opportunities for beginning teachers. The entry stage provides initial and ongoing assistance during the first two years of employment. A description of Parkway's staff development program designed for teachers in their first and second years of teaching follows.

Charting Your Course: A Five-Day Teacher Orientation

Beginning teachers take their first steps on the journey to become career educators by gaining a clear understanding of professional expectations; familiarizing themselves with the district; and "charting their course," the theme of a five-day orientation. All teachers new to the district are expected to participate and are paid a $75 daily stipend for their involvement.

The planning and delivery of the orientation involve a large number of district veterans who address two questions: What does it mean to be a teacher in Parkway? What is so important to beginning teachers that it cannot be left to chance? An integral part of each day of the orientation is a deliberate intent on the part of all presenters to focus on what is highly significant to teach and to demonstrate effective instructional strategies to help beginning teachers add to their repertoire of instructional techniques.

Day One

The five-day orientation begins with a welcoming breakfast for principals and new teachers, an address about planning for success by the superintendent, and an introduction to Parkway's expectations for professional teachers. Following a celebratory lunch that includes all administrators, new teachers have a chance to reflect and to set goals in a professional journal and to immerse themselves in their own copies of Harry and Rosemary Wong's *The First Days of School* (1998), gifts to them from the district.

Days Two and Three

During the second and third days of the orientation, participants "pack for their journey" and learn "expectations for the journey" by becoming actively involved as a community of learners. Teachers create plans for setting up their classroom community and share best practices about classroom management. Personnel from Human Resources and Student Development present vital information about key policies and laws. The teachers learn about the Performance-Based Teacher Evaluation process from an area superintendent. On two afternoons, curriculum coordinators introduce new teachers to Parkway's curriculum frameworks, outline content and instructional standards, and facilitate sessions on lesson and unit design.

Day Four

On the fourth day of the orientation, new teachers learn about the district's "life preservers" for students, such as support from social workers, security resource officers, health services, and the district's "Earn Your Way Back" program for suspended students. They learn how to intervene to support all students. Presentations from the departments of Special Services and Student Development and a volunteer panel of teachers, counselors, and nurses give participants guidance about ways to help each student realize academic success; Individualized Education Plans; and the Care Team, a group assembled from counseling and special education services, building administration, and faculty to assist students when serious concerns surface.

For one orientation, high school students, organized by members of the District Multicultural Study Group, presented their perspectives on how to embrace all cultures to make each student feel a part of the classroom and the school. The students' captivating descriptions and honest answers to teachers' questions touched many in the room and provided a voice for students' views.

Day Five

On the final day of orientation, veteran teachers, who are selected by their principals to serve as mentors, come to the Student Development Center to greet their assigned teachers, the new hires with no teaching experience. They are joined by all new teachers for a breakfast and a chance to ask final questions of some of Parkway's best. After an uplifting bon voyage from the superintendent and some warm words of congratulations from the president of the Board of Education, all teachers return to their assigned schools for a building orientation, with each mentor accompanying his or her assigned beginning teacher.

Amid an enthusiastic appraisal by all participants, the beginning teachers' reactions to what it means to be a Parkway professional are positive:

> The orientation was phenomenal. Although I was obviously nervous about my first few days of teaching, after the orientation I knew I had a support network that I could call upon.

> As a new teacher, I think support is so important. They also taught us a variety of teaching techniques, many of which I have already used. I think my students are benefiting because I attended the orientation.

Mentoring Beginning Teachers: A State Law and a Parkway Expectation

In accordance with Missouri guidelines, Parkway pairs outstanding veterans with beginning teachers. Principals identify and ask career teachers to serve as mentors on the basis of experience, demonstrated success, positive attitudes, and, when possible, certification and grade level.

The district offers mentors training opportunities in paid summer workshops and in a release-day workshop, which focus on developing conferencing skills and peer coaching abilities as well as on gaining knowledge about updated state certification and mentoring requirements. Mentors receive manuals replete with necessary forms, explanations of certification requirements, and details of available resources. The district provides release days for the mentor to visit his or her assigned teacher's classes, the beginning teacher to observe the mentor, and the mentor and beginning teacher to meet.

As new teachers acclimate to school and district procedures, mentoring promotes the ongoing support necessary to help new professionals increase their effective teaching strategies, problem-solving approaches, and skills related to curriculum and instruction. Mentors also help new teachers interpret the culture of their school, avoid isolation, and understand district and community expectations.

New teachers appreciate the guidance and the support they receive from their mentors, which include both professional and personal assistance. A middle school teacher remembers the 10 p.m. call to his mentor, whose words eased his fears. A young elementary teacher claims that peer teaching with her mentor was invaluable to her development of lesson transitions. Another mentions that he had no strategies to help a troubled student until he explored alternatives with his mentor. Receiving free access to the teaching files of a veteran teacher helped a beginning teacher cope with three different preparations. One high school teacher decided to try another year in the classroom after sharing his frustrations with the reality of his first year; his mentor encouraged him by offering the perspective of a teacher who still loved the profession after years as an educator.

Promoting a Learning Community: The Beginning Teacher Connection

By offering a series of after-school sessions throughout the year, Parkway staff development facilitators provide ongoing support for beginning teachers. During the Beginning Teacher Connection meetings, new teachers network and share instructional ideas, focus on practical topics that promote growth as an educational practitioner, work with district personnel and familiarize themselves with district resources, and partially fulfill Missouri's staff development certification requirement of 30 hours of professional development. Although all teachers new to the Parkway district are invited to attend, all beginning teachers are expected to participate in the after-school meetings.

One year's topics for the seven Beginning Teacher Connection meetings were Developing Your Professional Growth Plan (a district and state requirement), Planning for Successful Parent Conferences and Interactions, Establishing Effective Classroom Management Strategies, Providing for Differentiated Instruction and Abilities Awareness, Exploring Instructional Strategies and Lesson Design, Examining Multicultural Issues in the Classroom, and Familiarizing Yourself with Parkway Curriculum Frameworks. In addition, opportunities for grade-level discussions give teachers a chance to share age-appropriate suggestions for real classroom situations.

Embedding Professional Development in the Classroom: Videotapes and Observations

District staff development facilitators visit each beginning teacher's classroom twice during the first year of teaching: once to coach and once to videotape to promote self-analysis and professional reflection. The facilitators, career teachers who cycle into two-year staff development positions, emphasize that the visits should assist new educators in gaining experience as reflective practitioners, not be used for evaluation purposes. Each beginning teacher determines the schedule for the observations, and all written comments as well as the videotape are given directly to the teacher for professional reflection.

As teachers observe their videotapes, they reflect on their behavior and their students' responses with the help of a district-provided reflection form. They also analyze the positive aspects of the lesson and set goals for future lessons.

Each teacher's professional portfolio contains the videotapes and any written self-reflections; further videotaped sessions and analyses are included as the teacher progresses through Parkway's professional development program. Because each first-year teacher files a Professional Growth Plan with the staff development facilitators, classroom visits and follow-up coaching sessions can nurture an individual's area of focus for personal growth. As the facilitators gain firsthand knowledge of beginning teachers' experiences in the classroom, their visits also measure how well the teachers are implementing the topics covered during the New Teacher Orientation and the Beginning Teacher Connection meetings as well as how successful the mentoring arrangements are.

Evaluating: Planning for the Future

Questions of accountability accompany the district's significant commitment of time and resources to beginning teachers: Are we accomplishing our goals? Are participants profiting? Are students benefiting? Can the costs be justified?

Based on Thomas Guskey's (1998) model for determining the effectiveness of staff development programs, formative and summative evaluations influence the future of the New Teacher Orientation, the Beginning

Teacher Connection meetings, and the staff development facilitator classroom visits. Beginning teachers have, for the most part, enjoyed their participation in workshops and have expressed through evaluations and informal feedback that they have learned practical classroom applications, satisfying Guskey's first two levels of "Participants' Reactions" and "Participants' Learning." The Board of Education's support and reallocation of money for the induction effort, along with widespread district involvement in the planning and delivery of the orientation programs, indicate alignment with and evidence of Guskey's third level, "Organizational Support and Change." Through the ongoing, site-based support by staff development facilitators, Level 4—"Participants' Use of New Knowledge and Skills"—can be assessed in classroom visits and videotaped lessons. Observations and interviews with beginning teachers give evidence of the impact of the orientation, after-school staff development sessions, mentoring assistance, videotapes, observations, and coaching sessions.

Evidence of participants' reactions, direct classroom application, and the quality of implementation will guide revisions of future New Teacher Orientation sessions and Beginning Teacher Connection meetings. To answer the question of most significance—What is the impact on students?—evidence becomes more difficult to collect, however. Although the district has not yet gathered documentation of Guskey's Level 5, "Student Learning Outcomes," it possibly could use measures of student performance in beginning teachers' classes, compared with performances of comparable groups of students with beginning teachers in previous years, to evaluate return on investment. Student surveys furnish another avenue to see whether teachers are making classroom applications and how students react. The planning group, which encompasses a number of district resource specialists, will address this question as well as ways to gather evidence to improve the program design and delivery for Parkway's future new teachers.

Achieving Student Success Through Teacher Success: A Parkway Goal

"Our greatest contribution is to be sure there is a teacher in every classroom who cares that every student every day learns and grows and feels like a real human being," states Donald Clifton of the Gallup Organization (Miller, 1998). The knowledge, skills, and attitudes with which new teachers approach their classes influence students' capability and willingness to learn. Giving a new teacher a solid foundation is essential to establish effective instructional habits that could affect student achievement in that teacher's classroom for 30 or more years.

Supplying district encouragement for networking with other new teachers and district resource personnel enlarges the safety net and the resource web for new teachers and lays the groundwork for supportive professional relationships that may continue for decades. Providing an effective induction for beginning teachers requires a large commitment in time and resources, but it is an investment that can pay off in quality instruction for the duration of a teacher's career.

We now ponder the year 2029. Are we closer to fulfilling our mission that in every classroom, every day, every student can expect an excellent education? We believe that we are. Through the design and delivery of an extensive professional development program tailored specifically for beginning teachers, our students will reap benefits for decades.

References

Miller, J. A. (1998, June). Leaders as developers of people. Summer Leadership Institute, Parkway School District, St. Louis County, MO.

Guskey, T. R. (1998). The age of our accountability. *Journal of Staff Development, 19*(4), 37–43.

Wong, H., & Wong, R. (1998). *The first days of school*. Sunnyvale, CA: Harry K. Wong Publications.

Barbara Moore is Staff Development Facilitator for Parkway School District at Parkway South Middle School, 760 N. Woods Mill Rd., Manchester, MO 63011 (e-mail: bmoore@pkwy.k12.mo.us).

PART V

IMPROVING INSTRUCTION AND COMMUNICATION

Encouraging Innovation in an Age of Reform

Jeffrey Frykholm and Margaret R. Meyer

A model that unites preservice and inservice mathematics educators may be useful to all who prepare teachers—no matter what the discipline or field.

A close examination of today's school mathematics reveals two faces. One face looks to the future with a vision articulated by the *Standards* documents of the National Council of Teachers of Mathematics (NCTM, 1989, 1991, 1995). New goals for mathematics curriculum, pedagogy, and assessment are based on such ideas as problem solving, mathematical connections, mathematical communication, higher-level reasoning, and technology applications. To meet this vision, recently developed curriculums require new methods of teaching and new ways of assessing student understanding. Moreover, the *Standards* documents challenge teachers to reassess what mathematics is, what it means to know and do mathematics, and how we can teach mathematics more effectively.

The other face of mathematics education uses the lessons of the past to inform its vision. The curriculum, pedagogy, and assessment practices that characterize most of today's classrooms are essentially those that were in place when today's teachers were students of mathematics themselves. Many teachers, reinforced by curriculum guides and textbooks that emphasize skills and repetition, teach what they were taught, the way they were taught.

The typical mathematics class session has been well documented (Weiss, 1995; Welch, 1978; Frykholm, 1996): Class begins with questions about and answers for the previous night's homework, followed by a 10- to 15-minute teacher presentation on new material. Students spend the rest of class time working on the next homework assignment while the teacher circulates around the room giving individual help. Tests and quizzes reflect this pattern of instruction because they typically consist of short-answer problems that ask students to show that they have acquired the skills covered in the unit.

Educators responsible for preparing new mathematics teachers must understand these two faces of school mathematics. Moreover, they must recognize the people involved in teacher preparation and identify the faces they wear as they view mathematics teaching and learning.

Key Players in Teacher Preparation

University mathematics educators are directly involved with the initial phases of the preparation process. Their work with prospective teachers typically includes teaching methods classes and coordinating field placements. Throughout the preparation process, teacher educators attempt to shape the preservice teacher, often by sharing recent ideas in curriculum, pedagogy, and assessment reforms. One challenge in doing so, however, is finding a balance between the vision of mathematics teaching they believe in and the need to prepare teachers for survival in today's schools.

It is important for beginning teachers to closely examine, and in many cases broaden, their belief and knowledge structures. However, teacher educators must also be mindful that what they share with students in the university setting is not always reflected in school classrooms. Even as they encourage beginning teachers to adopt reform-based thinking and practices, they must help their students develop the tools and dispositions that will lead to a successful student-teaching experience.

The student-teacher supervisor is the second significant university presence in the preparation process. The supervisor's role is usually assumed by the instructor of the methods course, by adjunct faculty, or, at larger institutions, by doctoral-level graduate students. In any case, the role of the supervisor is a difficult one.

Supervisors are asked to represent the university and to advocate the goals and vision promoted in the methods courses, but they must do so within the context of the school setting *and* in the classroom of an experienced teacher. Because they are guests, they must be careful not to criticize either the school program or the cooperating teacher. Therefore, supervisors must delicately negotiate among the positions represented by the university, the student teacher, and the cooperating teacher.

Moreover, they must also carefully monitor the feedback they give as they remain mindful that student teachers must become comfortable with classroom management and other basic teaching skills before they can try innovative approaches.

Mentor teachers play a pivotal role in the preparation of new teachers. They are usually committed to their profession and to its future, and they often accept the responsibility of mentoring beginning teachers with little compensation. Again, the role of the mentor teacher is one of balance. Mentors must oversee the gradual process in which student teachers assume control of the classroom. At the same time, they must be attentive to the needs of their students, to the guidelines for content coverage and assessment, and to parental concerns. Even as they attempt to remove themselves from active roles in the classroom (thereby increasing the authenticity of the student teacher's experience), they remain the teacher of record and must assume responsibility for what takes place within the classroom. Hence, mentoring, or cooperating, teachers find it difficult at times to relinquish full control to student teachers for fear that later they will have to "pick up the pieces."

Because of the demands of their work and their many responsibilities, it is not uncommon for mentor teachers to become isolated from the ideas of mathematics education reform—particularly those promoted in the university methods courses. Cooperating teachers often must reconcile their own craft knowledge and practices with those that the teacher-preparation program has encouraged the student teacher to adopt. Finding the balance between mentoring and guiding student teachers and allowing them the space to develop their own ideas and practices about mathematics teaching can be difficult.

Student teachers, perhaps, play the hardest role among the participants in the preparation process. They are at a critical transition point in their lives. After spending years in the classroom in anticipation of becoming teachers, they are faced with a defining experience—student teaching—that will essentially determine whether they made an appropriate career choice. Although they are still students themselves, they are expected to perform like professionals.

Moreover, student teachers need to satisfy what are often conflicting expectations from university personnel, their mentor teachers, and students. They are conscious of wanting to fit in and be liked by both colleagues and students (Campbell & Wheatley, 1983). Classroom management is often difficult for student teachers, many of whom are only a few years older than the students they are teaching. Even when management is under control, pedagogy can remain a challenge because they have rarely experienced mathematics teaching and learning the way the university program promotes. Moreover, the teaching recommendations of university professors and supervisors often conflict directly with those of the cooperating teacher.

Promoting Common Ground

The many facets defining the preparation process at times appear complex, if not overwhelming. As Zeichner has noted, the lessons of experience for student teachers often seem to be "determined by the luck of the draw" (1996, p. 219).

In the face of these challenges, many mathematics educators continue to ask important questions about teacher preparation. How can we create preparation experiences that equip beginning teachers with the knowledge, skills, and habits of mind that lead to effective teaching? How can we strengthen our relationship with mentor teachers to minimize the disparity between the reform visions presented in the preparation program and the realities of the classroom? How can we offer more effective supervision and meaningful evaluation of our student teachers? In short, how can we find common ground so that this next generation of teachers may enter the profession assured that their footing is secure and that their sense of direction is true?

Building on this metaphor of common ground, we offer the following model as one that we believe offers significant promise for bridging the gap between university and school classrooms, for redefining the roles and relationships of the players involved, and for mobilizing wider support for reflective teaching in our school mathematics classrooms.

Four primary forces—student teachers, cooperating teachers, university supervisors, and the university preparation program—significantly affect the development of beginning teachers during the student internship experience. For example, student teachers work closely with cooperating teachers, are typically evaluated by university supervisors, and are products of the university preparation program. But only during the student teaching experience do all constituents converge.

For preparation programs, cooperating teachers, and school placements to offer more supportive and successful experiences for beginning teachers, we need to find a way to increase the overlaps in the learning-to-teach process. As we find ways to bring these constituents closer together, we increase the likelihood that we can decrease the apprehensions and conflict that many beginning teachers experience.

A Model Program

In fall 1997, mathematics education faculty members at Virginia Tech implemented a new course titled "Secondary Mathematics with Technology." The course focused on the technological tools appropriate for secondary classrooms, such as graphing calculators, the Calculator-Based Laboratory, computer software, and Internet resources. We designed the course to have broad appeal and application across the mathematics education spectrum. We hoped to attract students from the undergraduate education program, the master's level licensure program, and the doctoral program.

In addition, we were especially interested in attracting practicing secondary mathematics teachers from the area, particularly those who were good candidates for working with our students in field experiences. We saw the course as an excellent opportunity to strengthen our relationships with local teachers as we shared with them recently developed research and technological tools that they could implement in their classrooms. We also saw an opportunity to share ideas about teaching, learning, and reform through the teaching strategies modeled in the course itself.

Perhaps our greatest interest was fostering relationships among these classroom teachers, student teaching supervisors (typically doctoral students), and our prospective teachers in ways unavailable in the traditional student-teaching model. We were hopeful that as our preservice teachers shared ideas and collaborated with veteran teachers on classroom activities and presentations, new relationships would emerge that would offset the traditional power differential and socialization patterns that so often mark the student-teaching experience.

As we had hoped, we were able to place several of our students in the classrooms of teachers who participated in the course. We followed these pairs (and, in some cases, triads that included the university supervisor who had also taken the course) as the semester unfolded. As we informally examined and evaluated the many interactions that occurred among constituents, such as collaborations in the technology course, lesson observations, postlesson conferences, e-mail correspondences, and back-to-campus seminars, a number of interesting and notable preliminary findings emerged.

Participant Reactions

Although we did not conduct a rigorous research study, our informal reflections and anecdotal data point toward the potential and the promise inherent in this approach to mathematics teacher education. The following conversations and observations emerged from two cases in which the student teacher, the cooperating teacher, and the supervisor had been involved in the technology course.

Initially, the individuals enrolled in the course did not seem to be particularly concerned about, or even attentive to, the makeup of the class. As one student teacher noted,

> I didn't think too much about the makeup of the class at the time. There were undergraduate students, graduate students, and teachers in the class. I noticed the wide variety of ages and experience levels, but for the most part, I just viewed this as another class where everyone brings different experiences to the class.

As the course developed, however, it became quite clear that these "different experiences" would have an impact not only on the direction of the course itself, but also on the relationships that emerged among the participants.

The practicing teachers brought a pragmatism and a wealth of craft knowledge to the course that did not go unnoticed by the preservice teachers. As one course participant remarked,

> They [teachers] were the ones who were more likely to ask questions and be critical of everything we did. Most of the undergrads with no teaching experience were more likely to just take in all the information and listen to the experiences of the teachers.

The practicing teachers also recognized this opportunity to share their experiences and to provide, as one said, a "dose of reality" to the class discussions, small-group conversations, and activities that focused on how technology might be received and implemented by students.

The technology course had a heavy mathematics component that gave the preservice students an excellent opportunity to meet the practicing teachers on equal footing. The students and teachers worked together in a nonthreatening way and established a give-and-take relationship. One student noted that,

> At the beginning, I viewed them [practicing teachers] as the "adults" of the class. But as I worked in groups with them, I gained more confidence and felt as though I was more on their level at the end of the class. . . . By the end of the class, I felt completely at ease.

Evolving Relationships

The many interactions, discussions, and collaborative projects facilitated the development of relationships among the participants. We intended to watch the emerging relationships in the course and then assign placements as positively as possible on the basis of interests, personalities, and communication styles. Two of the inservice teachers beat us to this task, however, when they asked whether we could place students in the course with them for the following semester.

Once our student teachers realized that they would be working in the classrooms of these teachers in the spring semester, the relationships took a significant turn. The preservice students became much more sensitive and focused in their collaborations with their future cooperating teachers. As one student mentioned,

> When she told me that she thought that I was going to be her student teacher, it definitely had an effect on our relationship and my attitude toward the class. . . . I really enjoyed being in her group because I had so much to learn. . . . I was more inclined to listen to her stories about her school experiences because these were the students that I very likely would be teaching in the spring. Plus, I was definitely trying to make a good impression on her! I guess what I am saying is that knowing that I was going to be her student teacher, I really tried to learn from her.

The early identification of the student teacher–cooperating teacher pairs also led the practicing teachers to engage in the relationships differently. They began to prepare their future student teachers by describing the characteristics and tone of the school environment and of their classrooms. They began to think about how the course could help them plan for the various teaching responsibilities that the student teachers would assume. For example, one student described an activity involving a motion detector in which her future cooperating teacher encouraged her to do much of the work herself as a preparation experience for the classroom. She noted,

> During one class, we brought in the TI calculator lab where you race the cars up the ramp. We worked on it together, but Mary made me do everything because she told me that I would do this very lab in the spring with her kids.

Given how Mary used this activity to prepare her student teacher for the coming semester, the technology course appeared to hold the promise of promoting collaboration and innovative teaching methods in the classroom.

The Student-Teaching Experience

The technology course allowed student teachers, cooperating teachers, and supervisors to start the student-teaching semester with established working relationships. As one student teacher noted,

> Because we had the class together, we didn't have to take the "get to know you" time, or that time when you are trying to earn someone's respect. We got to do that in the previous semester. I was not nervous at all about student teaching with Mary.

Moreover, we placed two student teachers from the technology course at the same school, which comforted the student teachers. As one remarked,

> I felt really lucky that I could have such a nice cooperating teacher. Plus the fact that I also knew Kathy [the second cooperating teacher], I felt as though I would have two supports at my school in the spring. How many student teachers can say that? . . . I think this whole experience showed us how important it is to have teachers at your school that you can count on. It was the four of us working together and helping one another.

The student teachers noted how they felt supported and challenged by their cooperating teachers almost immediately upon entering the field. Cindy expressed her confidence in this way "My teacher gave me lots of freedom to do what I wanted. I wonder if she felt more comfortable with me because she also knew me from the [technology] class."

Certainly, establishing good working relationships that allow a student teacher the freedom to develop lesson plans and a teaching style are not exclusive to this model. However, we found worthy of reflection the question that Cindy raised: "Could this be because she knew me from the class?"

Encouraging Innovative Teaching Approaches

Perhaps the most important question we could ask regarding this model is whether it results in innovative, collaborative work in the classroom that would not have emerged in more traditional models. A primary goal of the course was to influence the practices of both pre- and inservice teachers by sharing recent and innovative approaches to mathematical content and by modeling pedagogical practices that embodied the principles of reform. We were hopeful that teachers would learn new ideas about how technology could enhance the mathematical understanding of their students and also come to a shared understanding of how they might work together toward that end.

There is little doubt that the content of the course led to specific teaching approaches. Both student and cooperating teachers showed uncommon ease and facility with technology in the classroom. They adapted many of the activities from the university course for their high school students. Supervisors observed lessons that incorporated graphing calculators, Calculator-Based Laboratories, geometry investigations with the Geometer's Sketchpad software, and other tools and computer programs introduced in the university course. Two notable findings surfaced with respect to the use of these tools.

First, student and the cooperating teachers engaged in much discussion about how they could highlight technology in the classroom. In contrast to teachers in more traditional settings, these teachers showed little distrust of the technology or uncertainty about the importance of its implementation. Because both student and cooperating teachers were already comfortable with the activities and the technology, they could move beyond discussions about how to use the technology toward more substantive conversations about how the technology was affecting the learning of their students.

Second, the explorations and the inductive focus that were hallmarks of the university course found their way into the school classrooms. The cooperating and student teachers encouraged their students to explore inductively, make conjectures, cooperate with one another, and use the technology to ask questions that previously were not possible, as they themselves had done in the university course. The university course not only resulted in changes in *what* the teachers taught, but it also produced changes in *how* they taught.

Both changes were supported in part by the depth and the quality of the relationships between the cooperating and student teachers. Their work together in the university course not only promoted new teaching approaches in the classroom, but also supported the development of these beginning teachers in a powerful way.

Common Ground

Promising points of consideration emerged from our experiences:

Developing a mathematics education community. This model powerfully connects individuals across the mathematics education spectrum. The technology course offered an opportunity for conversations *among* mathematics educators with various perspectives instead of conversations directed *at* one another. It is rare that university-level professors, classroom teachers, doctoral-level student supervisors, and preservice teachers gather around issues central to the future of mathematics education. This model provided a unique opportunity to meld inservice *and* preservice teacher education efforts, thereby broadening the perspectives of all involved.

Socialization redefined: Fostering collaboration. Rich relationships that developed in the course continued to grow in the subsequent student-teaching experience. This is particularly significant given what we know about the powerful socialization forces at work on beginning teachers (Zeichner & Gore, 1990). By the very nature of the apprenticeship model that typifies the learning-to-teach process, student and cooperating teachers rarely engage in the give-and-take that characterized the interactions in the technology course.

It is important that the relationships between the student and cooperating teachers were well established *before* the students entered the school setting. They formed these relationships from mutual respect, not dependence. The initial days in the school setting, in which student teachers naturally depend on cooperating teachers for guidance and support, did not represent their first interactions. As a result, the confidence and security of the student teachers remained intact.

The technology course modeled the kinds of collaborative learning and teaching advocated in reform literature. As the student and cooperating teachers worked together on projects and activities, they participated in the kinds of collaborative learning so important for our classrooms. Authentic engagement is difficult to manufacture in methods courses.

Bridging gaps. Finally, this model suggests that we can bridge the gaps between university preparation programs and school classrooms. University-based mathematics educators often decry the teaching practices that are commonplace in our schools. Likewise, many practicing teachers are quick to point out that the reform visions promoted in ivory towers do not reflect the realities of life in school classrooms. This model offers a powerful site for a reconciliation of these perspectives. Through experiences in the course, both teachers and teacher educators recognized the extent to which they already agreed with each other. As they learned to understand their differences, real progress was made where it counts most—with beginning teachers in the classroom.

In addition, these common experiences shared by university professors, supervisors, cooperating teachers, and student teachers may help relieve the pressure to meet the varied expectations of different individuals that many student teachers feel. Preservice teachers are often caught between a rock and a hard place. They must earn the respect and satisfy the wishes of the cooperating teacher while responding to pressures to implement the kinds of instructional practices advocated in methods courses. Through common experiences, all parties work closely to further the quality of the internship by building on the ideas and the relationships that originated in the common course experience.

Refining the Model

We have presented anecdotal data and promoted assertions that we derived more from thoughtful reflection than from hard evidence. Nevertheless, our model is worthy of continued development and examination. We have suggested how to provide beginning teachers with the kinds of support and learning experiences that they need to develop the belief structures and habits of practice that will lead to powerful teaching.

Although our model needs careful scrutiny, it makes strides toward blurring the boundaries that have for years marked the teacher-preparation process. As prospective teachers, practicing teachers, and university-based teacher educators find footing on equal ground, the greater the likelihood of a teacher-preparation experience that does not rely on the luck of the draw but rather is strengthened by the collective spirit of everyone involved.

References

Campbell, P. F., & Wheatley, G. (1983). A model for helping student teachers. *Mathematics Teacher, 76*(1), 60–63.

Frykholm, J. A. (1996). Pre-service teachers in mathematics: Struggling with the standards. *Teaching and Teacher Education, 12*, 665–681.

National Council of Teachers of Mathematics. (1989). *Curriculum and evaluation standards for school mathematics*. Reston, VA: Author.

National Council of Teachers of Mathematics. (1991). *Professional standards for teaching mathematics*. Reston, VA: Author.

National Council of Teachers of Mathematics. (1995). *Assessment standards for school mathematics*. Reston, VA: Author.

Weiss, I. R. (1995). *A profile of science and mathematics education in the United States*. Chapel Hill, NC: Horizon Research.

Welch, W. (1978). Science education in Urbanville: A case study. In R. Stake & J. Easley (Eds.), *Case studies in science education* (p. 6). Urbana, IL: University of Illinois.

Zeichner, K. (1996). Designing educative practicum experiences for prospective teachers. In K. Zeichner, S. Melnick, & M. Gomez (Eds.), *Currents of reform in preservice teacher education* (pp. 215–234). New York: Teachers College Press.

Zeichner, K., & Gore, J. (1990). Teacher socialization. In W. R. Houston (Ed.), *Handbook of research on teacher education* (pp. 329–348). New York: Macmillan.

Jeffrey Frykholm is Assistant Professor at the School of Education, University of Colorado, Boulder, CO 80309 (e-mail: jeff.frykholm@colorado.edu). **Margaret R. Meyer** is Faculty Associate at the Department of Curriculum and Instruction, University of Wisconsin, Teacher Education Building, 225 N. Mills St., Madison, WI 53706 (e-mail: mrmeyer2@facstaff.wisc.edu).

Linguistic Coaching: Helping Beginning Teachers Defeat Discouragement

Paul Caccia

A new slant on coaching—which focuses on partnership, performance, and communication—helps novices through those particularly challenging first days. It also helps seasoned teachers improve their performance.

A major challenge for teacher trainers and principals is "the balloon goes up, the balloon goes down" syndrome that many novice teachers exhibit. They begin their first year filled with enthusiasm for their work and optimism about the learning they expect will take place in their classrooms. However, within a few days or even a few hours, the clash between what they thought running their own class would be like and what actually goes on has discouraged and demoralized many of them. These new teachers describe their interactions with students as an endless succession of failures and end the teaching day emotionally and physically drained. Some even quit.

Usually, the problems that new teachers complain about and the discouragement that they express have little to do with their command of the subjects they teach or their grasp of effective teaching methods. Most of them, thanks to their college training, are more than ready to handle those requirements of the job. But all this knowledge goes for naught because the new teachers haven't yet learned how to establish authority and rapport with their students. If they don't, they'll be miserable and their students won't learn. If they do, they can recapture their initial

Editor's note: This chapter was adapted from "Using Semantic Coaching to Improve Teacher Performance" published in *ETC: A Review of General Semantics*, Vol. 53, No. 3, Fall 1996. Reprinted with the permission of the International Society for General Semantics, Concord, California.

enthusiasm and develop the confidence and practical know-how they need to be successful. My responsibility as a teacher trainer is to make sure that they do establish authority and rapport.

The most effective tool I have found for achieving this purpose is linguistic coaching, a comprehensive system of communications training. By studying this technique, I learned to establish rapport with and motivate hard-to-reach students; I improved my ability to get cooperation from parents; and in class, I became a livelier, more engaging, and more creative teacher. Moreover, I developed a tolerance for stress and a capacity to think on my feet.

Because of these personal and professional gains, I was sure that I could effectively use linguistic coaching to give new teachers a greater sense of authority—that is, an increased confidence in their ability to handle a class and an increased capacity to learn from problems and develop more options for dealing with them. In 1990, I began using linguistic coaching as the basis for a mentoring program for novice teachers. The success of that program and of subsequent programs for both beginning and veteran teachers convinced me that linguistic coaching is a valuable tool. It helps teachers cope more effectively with stress, establish authority for themselves in their teaching roles, and improve their overall outlook and performance.

What Is Linguistic Coaching?

Linguistic coaching, also known as semantic coaching or linguistic ontology, is a system of conversational analysis and communication designed by Fernando Flores (Flores, 1982; Flores & Winogrand, 1986). This system places such basic semantic distinctions as facts and opinions within the context of the Theory of Speech Acts pioneered by philosopher John Austin (1962) and refined by his student John Searle (1969, 1979). Underlying their work is the premise that all speaking and listening can be categorized as some kind of action—stating, promising, requesting, asserting, declaring, deciding, replying—in which the speaker makes a commitment with the listener. In Austin and Searle's view of communication, the central actions involved in, say, constructing the Empire State Building included not only excavating, lifting, and hammering, but also making assessments, requests, offers, and promises.

Flores realized that looking at communication in this way opened new possibilities for helping people avoid misunderstandings and work together more effectively. He applied Austin and Searle's categories of speech acts to make practical improvements in training personnel, designing software products, and managing a staff.

Linguistic Foundations of Teaching Performance

I took my point of departure in linguistic coaching from Flores's approach: all speaking and listening arise from a pre-existing background of beliefs, attitudes, experiences, and emotions. Whenever teachers do their jobs—plan lessons, handle student misbehavior, interact with administrators and fellow teachers—they bring much more than their professional training to what they are doing. A host of personal and cultural interpretations influence teachers' frames of reference for understanding and reacting to each teaching situation. Some of these are valid and some are not. Invalid interpretations make it difficult for teachers to adapt and to perform effectively on the job.

Mike, a first-year teacher, believed that "strong teachers handle their own problems." For him, requiring any kind of outside help in managing a class, such as sending a disruptive student to the assistant principal, was a sign of weakness—evidence that he didn't have what it took to be a real teacher. If he couldn't handle classes on his own, he wondered, what was he doing in teaching? With this nagging question in the background, Mike struggled through his first weeks on the job. His perpetually closed classroom door symbolized his isolation from the expertise and support of his colleagues. Behind it, he battled to maintain order with a mix of sarcasm, argument, and manipulation.

For those of us who don't share Mike's beliefs, it's easy to see how they could hinder his efforts to teach effectively. But because such beliefs and interpretations are part of the background that a teacher brings to the classroom, he or she either doesn't notice them or mistakes them for facts or truths that need to be dealt with in some specific way ("Tell me how you get them to keep quiet"). I am not saying that Mike or any of the other new teachers I've worked with didn't know the difference between facts and interpretations, but in my experience, we all sometimes blur this distinction as we go about the business of everyday living.

Making the distinction between facts and interpretations is an essential element of linguistic coaching: People cannot learn to communicate more effectively unless they develop this skill. Without the ability to make rigorous distinctions between facts and interpretations, they will remain blind to the personal obstacles they put in the way of achieving their goals and unclear about what they can do to act effectively.

Such lack of clarity often draws people into a hit-or-miss search for instant solutions to their communication difficulties, such as always saying something positive first or not taking things personally. Unfortunately, underlying interpretations at odds with the spirit of these communication techniques often undermine these approaches. By giving priority to externals—techniques and methods—many people try and discard one method of communicating after another. As a result, they get stuck in a fruitless struggle to reach some preconceived solution to a problem without recognizing that their difficulties stem from their perception of the problem itself—like people in the 1400s trying to figure out how far it was to the edge of the earth.

Mike, for example, wanted to know how I avoided being drawn into arguments with students. Even if I had given him specific methods, I doubt that doing so during Mike's first weeks of teaching would have had much impact on his overall effectiveness. Whether he argued or didn't argue, Mike's conception of his students—28 perpetual threats to his authority—would have stayed the same. To me, Mike's reliance on arguing and sarcasm wasn't the problem, but rather was a symptom of the real issue: being unaware of how his idea of strong teaching caused him to communicate with students in ways that perpetuated discipline problems. To help Mike become a better teacher, I had to deal with his underlying interpretations about teaching, not just get him to stop making sarcastic remarks.

Establishing the Coaching Relationship

Asking people to examine critically their underlying interpretations of things they care about is tricky business. Conducting this examination with Mike in a way that would help him better manage students required establishing a satisfactory working relationship with him. How free he felt to honestly share with me his thoughts and actions as a teacher and how open he was to listening to and acting on my suggestions were crucial to this relationship. I have found that the best context for fostering this type of relationship is coaching.

A number of fields, especially business management and education, borrowed the word *coaching* from athletics to name practices for improving professional performance. Some of these practices are little more than well-established teaching and management techniques dressed up with a new name. In many cases, the term is used interchangeably with *mentoring, demonstrating, instructing, advising,* or *supervising.* However, some innovators recognize coaching as an educational paradigm with unique features that promises to surpass traditional modes of teaching and training. They identify three elements necessary for effective coaching: (1) partnership, (2) a focus on performance, and (3) the communication of insights as opposed to information (Evered & Selman, 1989; Mink, Owen, & Mink, 1993; Delgado, 1994).

Partnership

The first element, partnership, calls for an explicit agreement on the part of the person being coached to be coached and on the part of the person acting as coach to coach. Even in my capacity as Mike's mentor teacher, I could not coach him unilaterally. As Evered and Selman point out, "no one can be coached in the absence of a demand for it" (1989, p. 21). Our coaching partnership depended as much on Mike's willingness to do something about his struggles as it did on my desire to help.

However, our mutual concern was not enough to create a good coaching relationship. If it were, I could coach all the teachers who approach me asking for advice. I'm not able to, though, because many of them lose interest as soon as I say something that challenges their perception of the situation they want help with. Coaching is not possible under such conditions.

To be coached, a person must first agree to be coached, that is, grant authority to, and act on the recommendations of, a coach in a particular field of performance. Committing to learn through coaching is the essence of the coaching part of linguistic coaching, just as making rigorous distinctions among facts, interpretations, and Austin and Searle's speech act categories is the essence of the linguistic part.

In making this commitment, the person being coached does not give up the freedom to express any doubts or concerns she may have about what the coach is asking. Mike, for example, often had reservations about what I said about discipline and authority. Although expressing such reservations is not a requirement of being coached, doing so can be the basis for more insightful coaching. By voicing doubt or disagreement, Mike let me see more deeply into the thinking that lay behind his actions in the classroom. In fact, his reservations became a frequent topic of our early conversations. The point of these conversations was not for me to sell Mike on my way of thinking or for him to defend his point of view. The purpose was to give me a clear picture of the interpretations behind Mike's teaching, reveal this background to Mike as the source of his teaching performance, and establish and develop our relationship as a coach and a novice in a partnership for learning.

The nature of this partnership sets coaching apart from mentoring. Unlike coaching, mentoring has no single, clear-cut definition for the roles of the parties involved. Some mentors describe their role as taking someone under their wing or showing a novice teacher the ropes. In this capacity, they pass along stories and anecdotes to illustrate lessons learned from experience. Others talk about their job as whipping new teachers into shape, a sort of stern taskmaster role. Still others speak of being available for new teachers, someone who will listen sympathetically—a confidant.

All these roles can have a positive influence on new teachers. However, defining these roles remains open to the discretion and the personal interpretation of the mentor and the mentee. Coaching offers no such leeway. It is an explicit partnership in which a coach offers insights and suggestions for the purpose of producing a specific, observable improvement in someone's performance in a particular field of action and in which the person being coached takes into account the insights and carries out the instructions of the coach.

Mentoring might involve coaching, but it can survive without it. For example, throughout my career I have served informally as a mentor to new teachers, who have told me how much they appreciated my observations. Flattered, I enthusiastically gave them detailed advice on a regular basis. And, just as regularly, they did almost the opposite of what I had suggested. In such cases, I was mentoring in the role of a favorite uncle—a sympathetic older person who expresses concern and patiently offers guidance in the hope that through his nonjudgmental but persistent concern, the younger person will eventually come around. There is nothing wrong with such a relationship; it's just not coaching, and, as such, has none of the incisive impact that coaching can have on professional performance.

A Focus on Improved Performance

Once Mike agreed to let me coach him, we moved on to the second element of effective coaching: a focus on performance. Traditional teaching emphasizes passing on new information or knowledge from teacher to student. Although a coach may give information, it's not the essence of what he or she does because a coach's primary focus is on improved performance, not just on intellectual understanding. I aimed everything I did with Mike at enabling him to embody new, more effective ways of communicating and to accomplish specific, observable goals.

Communication performance arises from our underlying interpretations of the world around us. I begin by making this premise explicit to the person I am coaching. For example, to deal with Mike's use of sarcasm and argument, I pointed out the connection between his manner of speaking and his underlying interpretations. Over the course of several conversations, I showed him that his understanding of strong teaching was just that—his understanding, not some immutable truth about education. Next, I asked questions designed to help him see how his idea of "strong" was the source of his "weak" performance: his reliance on sarcasm and arguments and the resulting ill will and lack of cooperation from his students. Finally, I suggested a different interpretation of strong teaching, one that included asking for help, making mistakes, and learning from those mistakes. In asking Mike to try this new interpretation with his students, I warned him that this new interpretation would be difficult to use and that it wouldn't feel strong at all but would gradually help him develop the authority he desired.

Each time Mike reported back, I asked him to state the relevant facts ("A student slammed shut her notebook as I was about to check her work"), his reaction ("I was mad. I thought that she was trying to make me look bad"), and his subsequent response ("I made a sarcastic remark"). I used his comments as a basis for coaching him to develop alternative interpretations and to take more effective actions.

In the notebook incident, for example, Mike's use of sarcasm arose from his premise that a teacher should "never let students know they got to you." I pointed out how this premise led him to resort to sarcasm and to be thrown off his purpose of checking notebooks. What alternatives, I asked, might he have employed if it had been OK to let the student know that she got to him? He agreed to try these alternatives in a follow-up conversation with the student. After speaking with her, Mike told me that being free to acknowledge that he had been upset put his conversation with her on an entirely different footing. Instead of, as he said, "playing mind games," he had been able to tell her frankly what he did and did not want. As a result, he was able to listen to her version with an open mind.

The point of my coaching was not to establish rules about communicating honestly or avoiding sarcasm. Rather, my goals were to show Mike how his thoughts and emotions affected his style of communicating, to offer an evaluation of how his way of communicating influenced his efforts to achieve his purpose, and to give him options for communicating more effectively.

A Focus on Communicating Insights, Not Information

The third essential element of linguistic coaching is the manner in which coaching conversations are conducted. Whatever I expected Mike to do with others, I had to do in my conversations with him. As Delgado (1994) points out in her training manual for communications coaches, coaching someone to communicate more effectively is communication; it doesn't take place in conversational quarantine, isolated from the requirements and potential pitfalls of everyday human speaking and listening.

For example, at times during our coaching conversations, something Mike did or said made me think that he wasn't taking me seriously or that I was boring him. Rather than pretend that I had no such reaction or simply to complain about Mike's lack of interest, I included my concerns as part of the coaching by stating my thoughts and emotions in a straightforward manner.

In doing so, I had three objectives. First, I was taking care of my duties as a coach. I needed to recognize and be responsible for my own actions, not just to react out of annoyance or worry. Second, I was showing Mike how effective communication depends on developing a greater awareness of the influence of our own backgrounds on how we listen to others. Third, I was modeling a particular mode of communicating that I wanted him to learn: reporting as opposed to pretending, accusing, or employing sarcasm.

Continuing, I followed my report by asking him questions about his background: Was he not taking me seriously? Was I boring him? Regardless of his response, my questions and Mike's answers engaged us in an alternative to the common mistake of assuming that we know the motives behind what the other person is doing. Finally, I made whatever request, promise, or offer seemed most likely to get us back to the purpose of our conversation—precisely the skill that I needed to refine to coach Mike and precisely the skill that he needed to develop to respond to student misbehavior without being thrown off track.

As the coaching continued, Mike became less sarcastic and more direct with students. He began to use routine discipline procedures, such as sending disruptive students to the assistant principal, instead of trying to manage everything on his own. Consequently, he had more time and energy to focus on teaching, and, as the year progressed, his strengths of organization, creativity, and compassion emerged: He formed a chess team, introduced innovative methods of teaching math and science, and counseled troubled students. These accomplishments were the result of the gifts that Mike brought to teaching, not of my coaching. However, the coaching allowed him to develop the resilience, clarity of purpose, and authority he needed to bring those gifts to light.

Outcomes of Linguistic Coaching

The three beginning teachers I coached during the 1990–91 and 1991–92 school terms achieved better results than their uncoached predecessors. The progress that the first participant made so impressed the principal that she offered him a second-year contract before the winter break. The following year, another beginning teacher was entrusted with developing a math and science program for academically gifted students, a job most often assigned to an experienced teacher. A third novice was offered and accepted a challenging second-year assignment in an inner-city school in New York, where she distinguished herself as a writing teacher. Whereas their predecessors had struggled just to get through the year, the novices I trained assumed leadership roles in the school community: one coached the basketball team to a long-sought-after championship, another began a chess program that was featured by the local media, and another organized and directed dramatic productions.

In accounting for their successes, the novice teachers all referred to how linguistic coaching had improved their teaching. One wrote,

> My acceptance of your offer of coaching has turned out to be the best aspect of our interactions for me. It helped me see the connection between what I think of myself and what the students (and others) think of me. You made me observe myself in a new way: I was able to see that I have certain ways of thinking and acting that don't get me the results I want, but that doesn't make me a bad person or even a bad teacher.

In the years following my initial work with first-year teachers, I have seen linguistic coaching improve the performance of administrators and experienced teachers. For example, a principal said that she learned to communicate with parents more effectively—to better manage complaints and to elicit greater cooperation—as a result of my coaching. A skilled veteran teacher reported that she enjoyed her students more because she had gained a greater capacity for not letting them push her buttons.

Linguistic coaching is also an effective tool for intervening in serious professional breakdowns, such as job burnout. When a teacher complained that he sometimes woke up on school days "sorry I'm still alive," I proposed that learning to communicate more effectively might help him overcome his feelings of frustration and powerlessness.

During the six months I worked with him, the burned-out teacher learned to communicate in ways that led to more effective action. For example, he began to participate in what he had considered to be "waste of time" faculty meetings instead of sitting in the back of the room reading the newspaper. He learned to make direct requests of students, parents, and administrators instead of airing vague complaints. As he tried my recommendations, his mood of apathy and hopelessness lifted. To his amazement, he began working late into the evening to create his own lessons, parents acknowledged him for keeping them informed about their children's behavior and academic progress, and his colleagues sought his advice on how to manage their classes as smoothly and creatively as he managed his.

The Ripple Effect of Linguistic Coaching

Beyond improving the performance and the outlook of the person being coached, linguistic coaching creates a ripple effect that benefits others. The principal and I found that the better Mike became at managing his classes, the less time we had to spend dealing with disruptive students, meeting with their parents, or handling the procedural details that go with enforcing school discipline. The workload of his fellow teachers became lighter because they no longer had to settle down students coming into their classes upset about some incident in Mike's room. Mike—like all first-year teachers—continued to have difficulties. However, neither he nor his colleagues got bogged down in endless repetitions of the same problem. His steady progress made all our jobs easier.

Also, the positive, goal-focused quality of our coaching conversations spilled over into our dealings with the principal, our colleagues, and the parents of our students. Many of them responded in kind. Meetings and conferences became more productive, and the faculty as a whole became more proactive in dealing with problems.

Of course, the biggest beneficiaries of Mike's improved communication skills were his students. Instead of wasting months or even a whole term—I've seen it happen—challenging the teacher for control of the class, Mike's students got down to the business of learning. As a result, their scores on national academic achievement tests exceeded expectations; their grades improved, as did their general attitude toward school and learning. All these benefits can be directly attributed to Mike's rapid transformation—through linguistic coaching—from an embattled, sarcastic rookie to a commanding, highly focused professional.

References

Austin, J. L. (1962). *How to do things with words*. Cambridge, MA: Harvard University Press.

Delgado, S. (1994). *"Coaching coaches" training manual*. New York: Delgado Consulting.

Evered, R., & Selman J. (1989, March). Coaching and the art of management. *Organizational Dynamics 18*, 16–32.

Flores, C. F. (1982). *Management and communication in the office of the future*. Unpublished doctoral dissertation, University of California, Berkeley.

Flores, C. F., & Winogrand, T. (1986). *Understanding computers and cognition*. New York: Addison.

Mink, O., Owen, K., & Mink, B. (1993). *Developing high-performance people: The art of coaching*. New York: Addison-Wesley.

Searle, J. R. (1969). *Speech acts*. Cambridge, England: Cambridge University Press.

Searle, J. R. (1979). *Expression and meaning: Studies in the theory of speech acts*. Cambridge, England: Cambridge University Press.

Paul F. Caccia is Principal of St. Thomas the Apostle School, 5467 S. Woodlawn Ave., Chicago, IL 60615 (e-mail: pcaccia@aol.com).

The Videoconference Connection

Ted Scott Henson and Kay Slattery Shapiro

In an effort to link new teachers and mentors in rural regions of North Carolina, educational leaders turned to video technology as part of a larger support program.

Lost mittens. Overly exuberant children. Stacks of paperwork. Too little time. Unfamiliar rules and regulations. Overwhelming grading problems. New communities and expectations. Too little money. State requirements for licensure. High-stakes testing. The burdens facing a first-year teacher are multitudinous and multifaceted. And when a beginning teacher is also new to a rural area, the challenges are multiplied.

How can novice teachers get help? Certainly, assigning a mentor to each new teacher is a step in the right direction. North Carolina, along with a number of other states, has established such a system. But how do mentors know how to help? They can provide a listening ear and a caring attitude, but what tools and techniques do they need to provide ongoing advice?

The North Carolina Center for the Advancement of Teaching (NCCAT) developed Connections, a program to help maximize the impact of the mentor–beginning teacher relationship. The Connections program, which the Center launched with a North Carolina school improvement grant funded through Goals 2000, uses videoconferencing technology to link the rural school districts of Robeson County and Vance County—two systems that have identified stronger support for beginning teachers and their mentors as a priority.

Helping New Teachers Thrive

North Carolina is not unique in losing many teachers during their first two or three years of teaching. If this loss of teachers is not reversed, the possibility of a state teacher shortage looms in the near future. The first year of teaching is pivotal in the teacher's future performance and longevity in the profession. Fuller (1969) and Katz (1972) refer to the first year as the survival stage of the teacher's development. The National Commission on Teaching and America's Future says in its report *What Matters Most: Teaching for America's Future* (1996),

> Turnover in the first few years is particularly high because new teachers are typically given the most challenging teaching assignments and left to sink or swim with little or no support. . . . Alone in their classrooms, without access to colleagues for problem solving or role modeling, discouragement can easily set in. (p. 39–40)

When schools provide trained mentors, beginning teachers are better able to focus on instructional issues much earlier in their development (Huling-Austin, Odell, Ishler, Kay, & Edelfdelt, 1989). Such beginning teachers become more effective because they are learning through guided practice rather than through trial and error and consequently have a much lower attrition rate (Darling-Hammond, 1994).

Dilemmas of Rural Recruitment

On the basis of this and other related research, NCCAT and the public school districts of Robeson and Vance Counties took on the challenge of lowering the attrition rate of beginning teachers. Although Vance and Robeson Counties are situated on opposite borders of North Carolina, the school districts share many characteristics. Geographically, the counties are quite large, yet their county seats are home to fewer than 20,000 citizens. Many school families in both counties are economically disadvantaged. And the student populations in both systems are quite diverse. In Vance County, 33 percent of the students are white and 63 percent are African American. In Robeson County, home to the Lumbee Nation, 44 percent of the students are Native American, 31 percent are African American, and 24 percent are white.

Several factors contributed to the high attrition rate for Vance and Robeson Counties, and both systems must hire more than 100 new teachers each year. First, despite aggressive recruiting efforts, the districts are unable to hire a sufficient number of teachers within North Carolina. Consequently, they recruit a large percentage of new teachers from out of state. Not only do these teachers face the familiar problems of all new teachers, but they also are separated from their family and social support systems. For many, this is the first major separation they have experienced. Second, the rural nature of the counties magnifies these problems. Many novice teachers feel isolated in their new settings. Most are able to adjust, but a few never make the transition that is necessary for a successful first year.

A Program to Connect New Teachers

To meet the needs of these beginning teachers and their mentors, the North Carolina Center for the Advancement of Teaching developed Connections, a program that uses a videoconferencing network to establish interactive communication among new teachers, their mentors, and NCCAT personnel. The Connections program had two major goals: (1) to show continual improvement in the retention rate for participating beginning teachers in these two school systems compared with that of beginning teachers not participating, and (2) to provide instructional support to increase the effectiveness of beginning teachers and their mentors within their classrooms.

To accomplish these goals, the program provided four major areas of support:

- *Videoconferencing sessions*. The Connections program used videoconferencing technology to link the school districts and the center, which are hundreds of miles apart. The initial grant funded this technology so that the cost to the participating districts was minimal. After working with local telephone companies to make certain that ISDN lines were available for the equipment, the program obtained technical training for a school employee at each of the three sites.

With a technically proficient staff member at each site, the program began broadcast sessions to connect the new teachers and their mentors. The sessions themselves addressed the unique concerns of the participating beginning teachers, such as classroom management, time management, instructional techniques, and assessment.

- *Structured time*. The program provided 12 days away from the regular classroom setting for interaction between the mentors and beginning teachers. Coordinators also encouraged the beginning teachers and their mentors to use the 90-minute breaks to have lunch together and strengthen their professional bond.

- *Strong support network.* The 30 participating beginning teachers, representing 19 schools, interacted with one another, their mentors, Regional Teachers of the Year, and NCCAT staff members. The participants networked closely with the people from their own county and made friends from the other participating county to create a strong support network.
- *Mentor training.* The newly developed Mentoring North Carolina Novice Teachers training program gave mentors three days of training. By participating in Connections, the mentors met the state requirement of at least 24 hours of training in a mentoring program. This strongly enhanced the mentors' skills and made them eligible for extra pay.

During the spring semester, intensive professional development was extended over 12 days. At the opening session, the morning was devoted to team-building activities so that the beginning teachers could become acquainted with one another's approach to education before the videoconferencing sessions. The activities made them less self-conscious when speaking before the camera. In the afternoon, activities were centered on determining the teachers' areas of concern.

To address these concerns, a team of five regional Teachers of the Year worked with an NCCAT staff member to develop the topics for each of the subsequent instructional sessions. The instructional topics included learning styles, multiple intelligences, classroom management, behavior management, differentiating instruction, alternative assessment, effective communication skills, and current educational trends in North Carolina. The last of the 10 videoconferencing sessions was used as a day for mentors and beginning teachers to apply the information they had gained to individual projects for their classrooms.

The videoconferencing equipment was set up in a central classroom in both school districts and at NCCAT. The NCCAT staff member provided instruction during the videoconferences and directed the exchange of ideas. Two regional Teachers of the Year served as local facilitators at each school system.

During interactive conferencing sessions, the teachers shared information related to the session topic with the teachers in the other system and with NCCAT personnel. Once the participants became familiar with using the equipment and seeing themselves on a big screen, the three-way dialogue began to flow freely. Questions and problems raised by the teachers in one system were often solved by the teachers in the other.

Toward Effective Instruction

Teachers participated in a variety of instructional activities. After identifying the individual student needs in their classrooms, the teachers described the ideal classroom to meet those needs. They discussed the barriers that prevented them from achieving the ideal classroom, and they brainstormed solutions. The groups then learned about methods to differentiate instruction. They chose a topic that they would teach and then designed activities to address different learning styles.

Hands-on activities were integral to the training. For example, teachers made paper cubes and wrote one activity on each face of the cube. One teacher wrote activities for a unit on the Wright Brother's flight at Kitty Hawk, North Carolina. The activity on one side of the cube asked students to construct a diorama of the 1903 plane at Kitty Hawk. Another side instructed the students to prepare a monologue in which Wilbur Wright told the story of the first flight. A third side asked students to compare the plane at Kitty Hawk with a modern plane. The teachers learned that by using a variety of methods matched to the unique needs of students, that they could differentiate instruction without doing 25 individual lesson plans.

Participants also discussed the importance of evaluation. They noted that just as a good photograph reveals details about the person in the picture, effective assessment gives important details about what the students know and are able to do at one particular moment. Traditional assessment tools, such as tests with multiple choice, true/false, and matching questions, were compared with alternative assessment forms, such as open-ended questions, essays, portfolios, presentations, and performance tasks. Participating teachers critiqued each type of assessment by asking the following questions:

- What would a student need to know to answer this question?
- What would I know about a student who responded correctly?
- What would I know about a student who responded incorrectly?

The teachers learned that using a variety of assessment tools gives a better picture of student achievement. Because rubrics are a fast way to measure overall quality, the teachers developed individual rubrics that could be used for evaluation in their own classrooms.

Teachers completed an inventory using the theory of multiple intelligences to identify their preferred modalities. They participated in activities ranging from singing math facts to dramatizing the lives of the Pilgrims to writing five key statements describing themselves. As they worked through the activities, they soon realized that for each individual, some activities were easier to learn than others. They applied this lesson to their students. By designing activities based on multiple intelligences, they helped ensure students' success.

The interactive sharing proved to be most beneficial to participating teachers. This was demonstrated during the final videoconferencing session, when mentors and beginning teachers chose projects to complete. During the video sessions, each pair shared what they were working on and asked for input. One pair shared a unit about the ocean. The other participants suggested related activities, such as building ocean dioramas and searching Web sites for information about ocean life.

Throughout the Connections program, teachers completed journals in which they reflected on what they had learned in each session. At the next session, they explained how they applied their new knowledge in the classroom. Then they analyzed the outcomes. Both the beginning teachers and the mentors participated in this process to foster continual improvement.

Improving Teacher Retention in Rural Schools

The results from the first year of the Connections program showed a significant improvement in the retention of beginning teachers in one school district and a slight gain in the other. In Robeson County, 80 percent of the participating beginning teachers returned for the second year, compared with a retention rate of 67 percent for all beginning teachers in the system. In Vance County, 72 percent of the participating teachers returned to the county, compared with 70 percent of all beginning teachers in that system. An even larger percentage of teachers remained in teaching but did not return to the same school system—86 percent for Robeson County and 90 percent for Vance County. These first-year statistics demonstrate the difference that this program makes in the retention of beginning teachers.

Participant evaluations revealed another important result of this project. A high level of trust and support developed among all the participants through their sharing. Not only did the beginning teachers experience growth, but the mentors also grew as a result of the enhanced mentoring process. Mentors mentioned that the variety of newly generated ideas helped improve their classroom instruction. They appreciated the ideas shared by novice teachers and felt reaffirmed about their own practice.

The program continues, and researchers plan to monitor its results over the next few years. In the meantime, Connections II, the second year of the program, continues to serve beginning teachers and their mentors—in an effort to ultimately improve the quality of education for the children of North Carolina.

References

Darling-Hammond, L. (1994). *Professional development schools: Schools for developing a profession*. New York: Teachers College Press.

Fuller, F. F. (1969). Concerns of teachers: A developmental conceptualization. *American Educational Research Journal*, *6*, 207–226.

Katz, L. G. (1972). Developmental stages of preschool teachers. *Elementary School Journal*, *73*(1), 50–54.

National Commission on Teaching and America's Future (1996). *What matters most: Teaching for America's future*. New York: Author.

Huling-Austin, L., Odell, S. J., Ishler, P., Kay, R. S. & Edelfdelt, R. (1989). Developing support programs for beginning teachers. In *Assisting the beginning teacher* (pp. 19-38). Reston, VA: Association of Teacher Educators.

Ted Scott Henson (e-mail: henson@wpoff.wcu.edu) is Center Fellow and **Kay Slattery Shapiro** (e-mail: shapiro@wpoff.wcu.edu) is Associate Director at the North Carolina Center for the Advancement of Teaching, 276 NCCAT Dr., Cullowhee, NC 28733.

Resurrecting Hope: Knowing the Facts, Imagining the Future

Anna Ershler Richert

When all the news seems bad, maintaining hope seems impossible. But by acknowledging problems, teacher-researchers can begin to understand and deal with them—and, ultimately, to resurrect the sense of hope that led them to the teaching profession

Hope is the physician of each misery.

—Irish proverb

I can think of nothing more important to the success of education than hope: parents' hope for their children's well-being, the community's hope for its schools' success in producing good citizens, and teachers' hope for making a difference in their students' lives. Many of us who work in and around schools understand the complexity of the enterprise of schooling in modern life and believe that hope is fundamental to the success of education. And so, in an era that seems to have lost faith—or hope—in public education, I see a need to address hope—how to foster it among teachers and how to resurrect it when it is lost.

I have learned a great deal about what I have come to see as a crisis of hope from my students who are teaching in the public schools of California. Their stories reveal not only the importance and power of hope but also the challenge of sustaining it. Diane's story provides one example.

Diane's Last Day

Diane was a student teacher in an Oakland, California, public school, and I was her teacher in the education department at Mills College. Diane planned the last day of her class for weeks. She baked cupcakes, made cards, and prepared a speech for her 7th graders. Diane wrote a personal comment for each of her 28 students. She intended to begin her last day with a speech in which she would recall an anecdote about each child.

"You will always be my first group of students," she planned to say. "I will never forget any of you."

As Diane described her proposed last day to me, she told me about Lance, who finally managed to get to school on time five days in a row, and Misubi, whose journal details of her boat trip to the United States gave Diane nightmares for weeks. She laughed about Tyrone's grandmother, who came to class and insisted that Tyrone sing with her before giving a talk about gospel choirs. She bragged about Pei-Wing, who figured out the mathematics of enlarging the class's mural to fit in the hall—even though she couldn't string together an English sentence. She brought pictures of Maria, whose project on chili tomatoes won third place in the district's science fair, an event that brought much pride to Portable No. 3 where Diane held her class.

I must admit that I felt relief as Diane told me of her plans to close the year. I had come close to abandoning my commitment to placing teachers in the city's often-troubled schools when one student was removed from Diane's classroom because he had a gun in his backpack and another student's brother was killed in a drive-by shooting near the school. That a hard year was ending made Diane's preparations for closing the year especially poignant.

Our conversation was filled with emotion. Diane spoke of what she had learned from each child and how she was learning to trust the human capacity to "transcend the struggles of everyday life." I thought about how necessary trust is for teachers and children in schools. Through her tears, she marveled at the genius of her students. I listened and marveled at the genius of mine. It had been a long, hard road for Diane. Juggling her own novice teaching skills in a setting beset with struggle, despair, hope, expectation, and love was almost more than she could bear. But she survived.

In spite of her careful planning, however, Diane's special day of celebration failed to materialize. Instead, as she rounded the bend into the school parking lot for her last day, she saw a pillar of thick gray smoke.

Tyrone was the first of her students to see her as she approached the back of the building that separated the main school from the 21-year-old "temporary" portables that housed close to one-quarter of the school's classes.

"Ms. D, we're in trouble," he screamed. "The portable's been burned down!"

Shock consumed Diane as she stood in the crowd of students and teachers watching the firefighters pull pieces of furniture from the ashes: desks, chairs, and the bookcase from the back of the room. Davis, her student from the Philippines, thought that he saw the desk he had carved his name on being pulled from the rubble. Diane felt Maria, the science fair winner, move closer and grab her arm. Occasionally Maria would heave a big sob.

"Too bad we didn't get here sooner," Diane tried to joke with her. "Maybe our tears would have stopped the fire. Do you know what happened?"

"The 8th graders were mad at Mr. Westin," Maria explained, "so they burned down his room. Ours went down with it. What will we do?"

"What will we do?" Diane repeated to me as she sat in my office. She continued her story, "I could think of nothing to say to Maria. I felt so lost."

This was not the first time that Diane was at a loss for an answer to a student's question. Nor was it the first time that I was at a loss for words to support a student of mine. I stood face to face with the stark reality of waning hope among the teachers that I know.

Sustaining Hope in Difficult Times

Although the burning of a classroom is not an everyday experience for teachers, it illustrates how vulnerable hope is—and how quickly it can disintegrate. Diane's story is not unique in its description of the conditions of many urban schools: overcrowding that requires portable classrooms; uncertainty that arises from teaching children whose language and life experiences are different from the teacher's; frustration and anger among students that sometimes leads to violent behavior; and painful events that can create a sense of helplessness and hopelessness for teachers.

Diane cares deeply about her work and about the students she teaches. However, she faces societal and school conditions that strongly challenge her ability to teach. But her experience after the fire opened unexpected avenues toward restoring hope.

Diane's students were one important source of inspiration; their care for one another—and for her—amazed her. They comforted one another in the face of their loss and talked about the importance of school in their lives. As they reflected on the fire and its impact, they expressed their desire to become more vigilant about making their school safe. The parents of Diane's students were also outraged by the fire and expressed sentiments about the importance of school that mirrored those of their children.

Diane's student-teacher colleagues provided great solace as well. They spent hours with her after the fire, discussing how schools must help students deal with their anger in productive ways and how significant relationships with teachers make this possible.

The entire experience was so moving that Diane decided to change her career plans and teach middle school instead of high school. She finished the year determined to take on the challenges that she and her student-teaching classmates identified as significant in their discussions of this painful yet inspiring event.

Creating a Context for Nurturing Hope

How do teachers hold on to hope, given the difficulties they face? What conditions in the schools and in the profession foster hope? I have garnered new insights about teaching and hope from a group of teachers with whom I work in a teacher research project on school change. More than 100 teachers have engaged in active inquiry about change efforts at their school sites. In the course of my study, the emotional and spiritual sides of school work and school change have become clearer to me.

Before I began to think systematically about the stories and other data from the teacher researchers, I read what Hargreaves (1997), Fullan (1997), Sarason (1990), and others had written on the emotional aspects of school change work. But not until I had spent considerable time with the teacher-researchers did I recognize the serious lack of hope for teachers. Through my participation in the research project, I now understand some possible mechanisms for restoring hope when it appears lost.

Restoring Hope by Providing Access to Change

My interest in hope and its connection to the teacher research project was sparked as the teacher-researchers began to analyze their material. Their data revealed in no uncertain terms serious problems with schooling and with school reform: Student scores were not going up markedly; poor children of color were performing in the lowest quartile; teachers were discouraged about the lack of progress toward reform. Yet, as the teacher-researchers reviewed their school reform data, I noticed an interesting occurrence: Contrary to my expectations, the teacher-researchers appeared more hopeful as the project proceeded, even though the data indicated little progress toward real reform and only slight (if any) improvement in student outcomes.

What alerted me to this seemingly incongruous reaction was my own response to the data: When I first encountered them, I had difficulty seeing beyond the bleak results. The teacher-researchers, however, responded differently: They were relieved. For the first time, they had a clear view of what was "really happening" in their schools. Amazingly, the data sparked a new commitment on their part to the work of change, a new capacity for doing it knowingly, and, consequently, a renewed sense of hope. How was this so?

For starters, the teacher-researchers were able to see more in the data than the simple numbers showed. In fact, the full composite of data revealed that the study itself produced positive indicators: Fellow teachers were happy to be asked about their ideas concerning reform; parents reported being more interested and knowledgeable as a result of being included in the survey; students became intrigued in their teachers' growing interest in what works and what does not. As I watched the teacher-researchers do their research work, and as I listened to them share many stories about change, I recognized how facing the truth can rekindle hope.

Karen's School

Karen's research offers a telling example of how one teacher revived hope by, paradoxically, collecting what appeared at first glance to be data that seemed anything but hopeful. Karen is a seasoned teacher who has spent most of her career teaching English in the high school where she conducted her research. At the outset of her project, she expressed substantial concern about what she saw as a collapse of morale among students at her school.

Her school is located on the outskirts of the San Francisco Bay Area and serves two widely diverse communities: a large immigrant population of children whose parents work in the agricultural industry of the area and the children of the landed wealthy on whose property the immigrants work. In presenting her research question, Karen explained that as the immigrant population grew at her school, and as the welcoming climate for immigrants simultaneously declined in the state, she noticed growing hostility among the students on her campus. There were more fights in the hallways and more expressions of racist and sexist sentiments in student writings for her class.

Karen began her study wondering whether what she perceived as increased racism and sexism on campus was actually occurring and whether other teachers also perceived this shift in attitude over the same period. She also wondered whether the various reform efforts at her school were having any impact on student beliefs and attitudes about race, class, and gender.

Karen collected data from a variety of sources. She reviewed materials that students had written for her class; she surveyed students about their ideas, beliefs, and feelings regarding different ethnic groups on campus—and about school life in general; she interviewed several students; and she surveyed her colleagues, interviewing several of them as well as the principal.

Her collected data presented Karen with a dismal picture indeed. Not only did the students appear to be racist and sexist in their views, but they were also even more racist than she had imagined, and more sexist as well. Although her colleagues were also alarmed at what seemed to be a growing tension among student groups, Karen found that no one was clear about what to do, and a good number expressed hopelessness in the face of community pressure and growing statewide anti-immigrant sentiment.

In spite of these findings, Karen gained energy for her work: "Ironically, as I collect more data regarding privileges based on gender, race, and class, I feel less defeated and vulnerable." She explained that standing apart from the problem in order to study it allowed her to piece together the puzzle more clearly and accurately. In turn, her understanding of the problem grew, and she felt for the first time free enough to begin to imagine how to address it. Before she had taken a systematic look at the situation at her school, she was consumed by it and unable to see her way clear to act. When the research took her out of the emotional midst of the problem and placed her in the position of being both an observer and an analyzer, she was able to experience curiosity about what really was going on. As she began to see more clearly, she felt a growing sense of hope.

Part of the clarity came from Karen's growing understanding of the superficiality of the students' rhetoric about race. As she listened closely to their words in follow-up interviews, Karen learned that their positions on matters of race were not deeply held. In fact, the students largely had little understanding of race and of the racial politics of their community. Karen found that in substantive conversations, many of her students were quick to abandon their opinions. As she learned more about what her students said and what they meant, Karen understood more clearly how she could teach them. The possibility of a new course of action renewed her sense of hope.

Joan and Arturo's Study

Joan and Arturo's experience gave me further insight into the value of inquiry in restoring hope, even when that inquiry reveals troubled conditions in schools. Joan is the head of the English department at a large comprehensive high school in the San Francisco Bay area; Arturo is a novice math teacher. As a research team, they decided to study one effect of California's reduced class size initiative, which began in 1992 in California's 9th grade English classes. Their research question was whether putting fewer students in a class affected writing achievement. Their data consisted largely of the writing scores of the 9th graders over a six-year period.

Joan was especially interested in looking at these scores in a systematic way. She knew "in her bones" that she could teach better with fewer students in her class. Having fewer students allowed her to respond more fully and quickly to their work, to listen more carefully to their comments in class, and to be more available when they needed additional help.

Arturo envied his colleagues in the English department and was eager to document the beneficial effects of this program so that he could argue for reducing class size for the math department as well.

When their data came in, the disappointment that Joan and Arturo felt was profound. Smaller classes had not resulted in improved scores; the writing scores did not change. As chair of the department, Joan was especially disappointed. But, as with Karen, the results sparked new interest that brought new direction and focus to her work—and renewed hope.

This path to hope was not easy or obvious, however. The discouragement that Joan and Arturo both felt initially was a response to the stark truth they were forced to face on reviewing their data. They had deep concern for their students, whose chances for success did not appear improved by a reduction in class size. They were also concerned for their colleagues, whose efforts had not yielded the outcomes toward which they had worked so hard. Moreover, they were sad for their students' parents, who had entrusted them to teach their children well.

To complicate matters, Joan and Arturo were afraid to call attention to the negative data. They were fearful that their results would lead to a reactionary response: Class size would go up, and support for reform would wane. Additionally, they were concerned that school colleagues, anticipating positive results, would question their credibility as researchers.

Despite these concerns, Arturo and Joan worked diligently to understand their data. One strategy was to place their findings in a larger context. They asked themselves about testing in general, for example: What do we know about tests? Is the writing assessment we use a good indicator of writing achievement? They asked themselves about demographics and its possible relationship to their results: What do we know about our student population over this six-year period; were there any significant changes that might help explain our results? They asked themselves about the reduced class size program as it was being studied across the state: What are other schools finding from their reduced class size programs? Are other schools learning something that might help us understand what our data show?

Many of Joan's teacher-researcher colleagues were studying the effects of class size reduction at their elementary schools. Joan noticed in her discussions with them that they emphasized changed pedagogy as an important corollary to smaller class size, something she had not considered. She explained, "When we reduced class size in English, we didn't talk about changing our pedagogy because we had fewer students. We simply taught the same way but with fewer numbers."

The conversation in our research group sparked Joan's thinking about how teaching writing might be different for smaller classes. Her insight led to a departmental meeting at which she presented both the negative data and her emerging idea about how the department could change the pedagogy of writing. Citing the work of her teacher-researcher colleagues, she initiated a conversation that led directly to the development of new teaching strategies and changed pedagogy for the subsequent spring semester. For example, Joan instituted a new program of peer review that gave students more feedback about their writing than she could provide on her own.

Before participating in the teacher-researcher conversations, Joan had operated under—and had not moved beyond—the belief that with fewer students, she could offer more feedback. She had not yet revised her thinking to consider the many new grouping strategies available for a smaller class. As Joan and Arturo discussed their data with both the teacher-researchers and their colleagues in the English department, they began to feel more hopeful that such changes would be effective.

Though the writing-score data for this year are not yet in, Joan and Arturo have begun to analyze the data they are collecting about teacher attitudes associated with these new efforts in the English department. Both teachers express new hope and enthusiasm. As Arturo said, "Teacher research is powerful because it gives you insights that you would not otherwise have." He added, "You can initiate change so that hope exists." As was true for Karen, when Arturo gained clarity about the situation at his school, he felt empowered to take new action.

Teacher Learning, Action, and Hope

> The test of a first-rate intelligence is the ability to hold two opposed ideas in the mind at the same time, and still retain the ability to function. One should, for instance, be able to see that things are hopeless, and yet be determined to make them otherwise.
>
> —F. Scott Fitzgerald, *The Crack-Up*

As teachers see possibility in the world where they work, and as they learn how to learn more about that world, they are better situated to act in new ways because they understand more fully the realities they face. Said one teacher,

> I am understanding better what's going on at school as a result of surveys, meetings, and informal talks with teachers. This gives me a better perspective of what needs to be done and what I can do to help.

And another corroborated,

> Through this project, I've learned to understand more about the process of change: its messy parts, its backward steps, and finally some little glimmering of positive movement. It has made me a more responsive and risk-taking teacher.

This risk-taking quality signifies a changed stance toward practice that is exemplified by Joan, who risked approaching her faculty with the sad results conveyed in the writing scores and her new ideas about changing classroom practice. It is what Arturo referred to when he suggested that new insights provide an impetus for initiating change.

Many of the teacher-researchers reported this willingness to initiate change. It is what connects many of them to a renewed sense of hope. Because of what they are coming to know more comprehensively and clearly about their school work, they feel confident to step into the uncertain and changing world of practice with new ideas, new plans, new actions, and new questions. One teacher explained,

> I don't have to do something one way just because it's an entrenched method. I can try something different, watch the results and modify it again, and watch the results and modify it again.

Being able to stop the action of teaching in order to ask questions and taking the time to pursue the answers systematically are essential to the process of changing attitudes and actions in teaching. As one teacher remarked,

> What I've learned from this teacher-research experience is that without the time to reflect and discuss concerns, there is little hope of changing anything within our school culture.

What I have learned from the Teacher Action Research Project is that when teachers engage in honest inquiry, even if that inquiry presents disheartening findings, hope arises. This engagement of teachers becomes a transcendent force for changing practice in individual schools and the world of education in general. When hope is resurrected and nourished, it connects teachers with the motives that brought them to the profession in the first place. When we resurrect hope, we resurrect the spirit of possibility, promise, and change for our schools.

References

Fullan, M. (1997). Emotion and hope: Constructive concepts for complex times. In A. Hargreaves (Ed.), *Rethinking educational change with heart and mind* (pp. 216–233). Alexandria, VA: ASCD.

Hargreaves, A. (1997). Rethinking educational change: Going deeper and wider in the quest for success. In A. Hargreaves (Ed.), *Rethinking educational change with heart and mind* (pp. 1–26). Alexandria, VA: ASCD.

Sarason, S. (1990). *The predictable failure of school reform*. San Francisco: Jossey-Bass.

Anna Ershler Richert is Professor in the Department of Education at Mills College, Oakland, CA 94613 (e-mail: AnnaER@aol.com).

Preparing to Teach in Holistic Classrooms

Kristin Guest and Jeffrey Anderson

Seattle University's Master in Teaching Program prepares new teachers to be holistic educators through collaboration, the arts, and service learning.

By challenging and encouraging their students, teachers invite students' awareness of the possibilities within themselves and of their ability to serve others. How can we prepare new teachers to have the knowledge, skills, and habits of mind to teach holistically and effectively? The Master in Teaching (MIT) Program at Seattle University brings these things within reach.

Picture these classrooms of MIT graduates:

- Janet Barks, Victoria Carver, and Devorra Eisenberg collaborate in designing and implementing a 9th Grade Academy, a team-designed, team-taught integrated curriculum.
- Meg Mahoney's 6th graders are studying endangered species. Their unit culminates in a series of dance scenarios narrated by students, who create and read from "interviews" with endangered species.
- John Traynor's high school students engage in service learning with urban social service agencies in Seattle as part of a social studies "Urban Plunge Weekend."

These beginning teachers were prepared in a program that has at its heart a holistic model of teaching (Miller, 1998). A central foundation of Seattle University's MIT Program, based on its Jesuit tradition, is that "we endeavor to assist our students to become knowledgeable, skilled, and confident; to grow in breadth of perspective and depth of concern; and to develop their spiritual and ethical talents." Feedback from principals suggests that program graduates are highly successful first-year teachers who move quickly into leadership roles.

Program Overview

The MIT Program, a 60-credit, four-quarter graduate program, prepares students to succeed as first-year teachers, helping them evolve from beginning to master teachers and leaders in their schools. Throughout the program, students move back and forth between university course work and work in schools, spending approximately 50 percent of their time in each setting. The program features multiple field experiences with strong supervisory support and incorporates peer collaboration with team-teaching approaches.

Students begin the MIT Program with a week of intensive study called "The Teacher As Reflective Decision Maker," which examines cultural, social, political, and ethical issues related to schooling in the 21st century. It also prepares students to be skilled observers in schools. After a two-week field experience observing schools, students gather for a retreat, "The Arts and Cultural Diversity."

In the first full quarter of the program, we alternate instruction in university classes on "Learners and Instruction" and placement with a peer coach in a school setting. All students begin the second quarter with a component on early adolescent development, instruction, and curriculum, as well as a middle school field experience. This is followed by a focus on methods for the elementary or secondary level, provided partially at school sites and taught jointly by university and public school faculty.

The next extended quarter focuses on student teaching, followed by a reflective teaching seminar during the final quarter. In this seminar, students complete a self-assessment and develop a professional improvement plan that provides guidance and support for their first year as teachers.

Throughout the program, we interweave applications of technology. In addition, all students carry out a group action research project; receive instruction in academic service learning; and participate in a service-learning project with K–12 teachers, students, and community members.

Four aspects of the MIT preparation are particularly important to the effectiveness of our training new teachers: a focus on collaboration, the arts in the classroom, preparation for Washington State's learning goals and essential learning requirements, and service learning.

Collaboration: Caring and Connection in Classrooms

Our teacher preparation program operates from the premise that if our faculty models collaboration and community, and if students experience these caring relationships, then students will be more likely to collaborate as beginning teachers and to create caring communities in their own classrooms.

Collaboration is essential to the entire design, delivery, and outcome of the MIT Program. Faculty members collaborate in course curriculum development and refinement, and most courses are team taught. Students proceed through the program as members of a cohort, which gives them the opportunity to create and experience a learning community.

During the first quarter, students work in cooperative groups as they learn about the theoretical basis of cooperative learning and apply strategies to their own lesson designs. To reinforce the idea that teachers can be excellent resources, we place students in their second field experience in peer coaching pairs to observe and give feedback to each other during their early classroom teaching. By working largely in groups both on service-learning projects and action research, beginning teachers learn not only to survive, but also to thrive during their initial years in the classroom.

As a natural outgrowth of our collaborative efforts, MIT graduates Janet, Victoria, and Devorra are piloting a 9th Grade Academy at Nathan Hale High School in Seattle. The Academy has team-designed and team-delivered instructional blocks, during which language arts, social studies, science, and health are integrated. Faculty teams meet daily to discuss curriculum and student progress. They foster community through service-learning projects and mentoring groups in which each faculty member mentors 21 students daily throughout the students' four years of high school.

Creativity: The Arts in Classrooms

Meg Mahoney's students use movement to understand and express their academic learning. This is another example of the MIT Program's holistic mission. Early in their teacher preparation, MIT students and faculty gather for a two-day residential retreat on the arts and cultural diversity. A cadre of experienced and skillful artists, who are also gifted teachers, engage students in music, movement, drama, and the visual arts, introduces participants to ways in which all the arts can be integrated into classrooms.

At the retreat, teacher candidates explore how movement can enhance academic instruction. To learn language arts, for example, they spell words with body letters and act out nouns and verbs. For social studies, students focus on dance elements from four countries and improvise dance with authentic music from these cultures. Students move in different counts to gain a kinesthetic understanding of number value in math, and they form geometric terms with body shapes. In science, students may create a cinquain about a scientific concept—for example, electricity or typhoons—and act out the cinquain through movement as it is read aloud. In addition, our dramatists help students "inhabit history" as they listen to a concise narrative of a historic event, identify the important roles in the event, and then explore the events through role play.

Through such experiences, teacher candidates' creativity explodes as they see possibilities for teaching with and through the arts. But perhaps the most exciting outcome of the retreat involves touching the spirit. At every retreat, a number of students, recalling with pain and tears past experiences that convinced them that they could not sing, dance, or draw, break through personal barriers as they risk expressing themselves through an artistic medium.

We continue to explore the arts at subsequent points in the program, and we encourage and model creativity. For example, students employ lesson-planning models that require them to address diverse learning styles and that involve active, concrete, intuitive, visual, and metaphorical ways of introducing concepts. For several assignments, MIT students have the option of synthesizing course themes and their own insights by writing poetry, composing music, creating a painting or sculpture, or shooting a video. These experiences allow program graduates to consider alternative means of performance assessment and to touch their own students' spirits through the arts.

Preparing to Address New Standards

Seattle University's School of Education, which houses the MIT Program, and three school district partners, the Everett, Northshore, and Shoreline districts, are involved in a pilot program funded by Goals 2000 and the Stuart Foundation to develop a program for beginning teachers. The pilot allowed us to assess the needs of first- and second-year teachers and to consider how the MIT Program could better prepare beginning teachers. The goal is to align preservice and professional certification programs.

Other districts across the country may also benefit from one of the outcomes, a matrix of knowledge and skills that articulates the developmental learning process of a teacher (Simpson, 1997). This matrix, on which a set of rubrics are based, guides instruction and assessment of student learning in the MIT Program through a performance-based model.

During the second quarter of the MIT Program, students preparing to teach in elementary and secondary schools develop unit plans on the basis of Washington State's "Essential Academic Learning Requirements." In these plans, students must identify specific learning targets and create multiple forms of assessments, including pretesting and posttesting. While student teaching, student teachers gather evidence from seven of their students, each representing a different level of performance, to document the positive impact that the student teacher had on learning. The student teachers' reflections serve as a basis for a professional growth plan in their first years of teaching.

Service-Learning: Caring in the Community

Within the context of a caring community, "Service Leadership" is a two-quarter credit course required of all new teachers in the MIT Program. The primary goal is to facilitate their understanding of collaborative efforts with the larger community through academic service learning.

Service learning integrates meaningful service to one's school or community with academic learning and structured reflection on the service experience (Krystal, 1998). This teaching method asks students to apply academic skills and content to the act of serving others.

While still an MIT student, John Traynor collaborated with teachers at Seattle Prep High School to plan and implement an intensive service-learning experience for 50 high school students. These sophomores were enrolled in two sections of a course that integrated world history, religion, and English. John collaborated with other teachers to implement an

"Urban Plunge Weekend."

John worked with students to explore ways to learn about issues of homelessness, poverty, and hunger and to contribute to improving the lives of people caught in these circumstances. The Urban Plunge involved two weeks of in-class study of these urban problems, followed by a weekend in which students spent more than 15 hours serving in homeless shelters, food banks, and other social service agencies in and near downtown Seattle. Students prepared and served food, socialized with agency clients, cleaned facilities, and ran errands at three homeless shelters. At night, all 50 students returned to the Seattle Prep gym where they slept on the floor in sleeping bags and reflected on their experiences.

Many students had emotional experiences during the weekend as they developed insights about and appreciation for the people they met. As the students reflected on what happened, the group expressed a commitment to work on underlying issues of social justice.

John was also deeply affected by the weekend:

> I find myself constantly looking for opportunities to incorporate service-learning projects in my classes. I believe these activities lead to enhanced empathy and improved citizenship, compassion, and community involvement.

MIT Service-Learning Outcomes

John's experiences are not unique. About one-third of MIT graduates implemented a service-learning project during the first year of teaching at elementary, middle, or high school levels, and 85 percent intend to do so in their future teaching. Their K–12 students have created a school garden; donated food to homeless shelters; written, illustrated, read, and donated books (in both Spanish and English) to childcare centers; tutored recent immigrants to pass citizenship tests; tested water quality and worked on adopt-a-stream projects; and learned many things while serving others.

While in the MIT Program, our preservice teachers have assisted more than 5,000 students, 60 teachers from 35 schools, and thousands of community members. Ninety-nine percent of the experienced teachers requested that MIT students return to provide more service-learning assistance in their classrooms, and we have a waiting list of school sites for placing our students. Most important, 21 percent of the experienced teachers said that they would not have attempted service learning without the MIT students' help.

Beginning and experienced teachers often find that service learning is a challenge to use as a pedagogy. To assist MIT graduates who are new teachers, we place many of our current students with our graduates for the 25-hour service-learning field experience. Collaboration helps our beginning teachers incorporate service learning into their teaching repertoire.

So the ripples spread. Through the themes of collaboration and community, the arts, performance-based learning, and service learning, MIT students prepare themselves to touch the lives of tomorrow's students. These new teachers kindle joy and meaning in teaching and learning, enabling their students to grow in breadth of perspective and depth of concern.

References

Krystal, S. (1998, December/1999, January). The nurturing potential of service learning. *Educational Leadership*, 4, 58–61.

Miller, J. (1998, December/1999, January). Making connections through holistic learning. *Educational Leadership*, 4, 46–48.

Simpson, M. L. (1997). *The professional standards matrix*. Bothell, WA: The Educational Resource Network.

Kristin Guest (e-mail: kguest@seattleu.edu) is Professor of Education and **Jeffrey Anderson** (e-mail: janderso@seattleu.edu) is Associate Professor of Education, School of Education, Seattle University, Broadway & Madison, Seattle, WA 98122-4340.

PART VI

LISTENING TO TEACHERS

Keeping Good Teachers: Lessons from Novices

Catherine M. Brighton

Going to the source—the new teachers themselves—helps us understand why they leave the teaching profession and what we can do to encourage them to stay.

Nationally, 60 percent of current teachers are eligible to retire in the next six years, which will leave many classrooms in urgent need of teachers. Other factors that affect an increased demand for teachers are growing school enrollments and state and national mandates to lower teacher-student ratios.[1] This need for teachers makes the high attrition rate among teachers entering the profession alarming. What can we do to keep these beginning teachers in the classroom?

My job is to mentor and coach teachers, many of whom are novices identified by their principals as needing support and additional training. I see beginning teachers face the challenges that cause frustration and job dissatisfaction. For example, Carly, a second-year teacher in a southern urban school system, works with me to gain additional classroom instruction:

> I thought I knew all there was to know about teaching children. I graduated with my masters' degree. My student teaching experience was really positive; I easily related to my colleagues as well as to the children and their parents.
>
> I knew there was trouble when my new principal started our first staff meeting with "you have the morning to move into your new classrooms" and all that I was moving into my classroom was in my backpack. I didn't know whom to ask or where to look for help, and I was so afraid of looking unprepared.
>
> The rest of the year I felt like I was running to catch up with my colleagues. At the second staff meeting, the principal asked volunteers to share the best thing that happened during the last week. The best thing was that I didn't cry in front of the children.

Carly is not alone. Studies suggest that frustrated by the demands of the job and the struggle to maintain control of student behavior, 30 percent of beginning teachers quit within the first five years; the attrition rate is often higher in urban districts and specialty fields.

Why Beginning Teachers Leave

Before we can suggest solutions to the problem of teacher attrition, we must understand why new teachers leave the field. Four major trends emerge from the literature as well as from the testimonies of novice teachers.

1. *The expectations and scope of the job overwhelm novice teachers.* Teaching is a difficult job even for experienced educators. Meeting the needs of all students in increasingly diverse school settings, efficiently handling the excessive paperwork, demonstrating time management, and negotiating in a political environment challenge the most savvy educator. Establishing positive connections between home and school are additional burdens for new teachers. Some parents communicate reticence about dealing with new teachers, fearing that they are largely unorganized, inexperienced, and unable to control student behavior.

2. *Novice teachers experience disparity between their preparation and the expectations of the job.* The student teaching experience is misleading because the cooperating teacher and the student teacher share job responsibilities. Administrators usually choose cooperating teachers on the basis of their demonstrated effectiveness and their willingness to mentor new teachers. Additionally, the student teaching experience typically begins after the cooperating teacher has established classroom climate, rapport with parents, and behavior and work expectations. The cooperating teacher supervises closely so that he is able to rescue the student teacher from lessons gone awry. The student teacher is easily lulled into believing that these elements will be givens in her future classroom. But no such safety net exists for first-year teachers.

3. *Novice teachers feel isolated and unsupported in their classrooms.* Education students are largely trained (including the practicum experience) in a collaborative environment in which teamwork, group activities, and brainstorming are emphasized. However, in real life, teachers are usually the only adult in a room of children during the instructional day.

The discrepancy between these two environments causes feelings of isolation and desertion. Further, veteran teachers sometimes view completing the first year of teaching as a rite of passage that translates into the belief that "if I could do it, you can do it. If you can't, you aren't as strong as I am."

4. *A gap emerges between novice teachers' expectations and the realities of the job.* Novice teachers are optimists, certain that they can change the world and the children in their charge. Many young people enter the field of education for the same reasons that others join the Peace Corps or other service organizations. They see their mission as shaping the lives and the minds of children. Once these idealistic teachers enter their classrooms, they are often discouraged that the work is so challenging, the children are so needy, and the expectations are so high. New teachers don't leave because of the difficulty, but feel disheartened that the reality is so different from their expectations.

Advice from Novice Teachers

By listening to our own novice teachers talk about new-teacher induction, we might learn the key to decreasing novice teacher attrition. The following solutions might keep new teachers in the field.

Solution 1: Provide nonthreatening feedback about teaching performance. A beginning teacher shared concerns about the teacher evaluation process at her school.

> I feel torn about taking risks. I am so eager to try new things, but I am afraid to not have everything go perfectly for my formal observations (the only time I get feedback from my boss). I don't want to fall on my face taking a risk, so I play it safe and do the boring whole-group lessons where I can keep total control of my classroom. I wish I could try new things and get honest feedback from someone who knows me and what I am trying to do.

New teachers seek opportunities for feedback about their teaching performance, yet are simultaneously afraid that administrators and supervisors could use this feedback against them. Some new teachers hesitate to ask questions for fear of looking inadequate. This contradiction often encourages a new teacher to play it safe in formal observations instead of feeling confident about taking instructional risks. Supporting new teachers with better feedback would benefit administrators. The success of the new teachers reflects positively on building administrators; conversely, teacher attrition is seen as their failure.

Solution 2: Give new teachers dedicated support from a mentor who isn't a colleague or a supervisor. Because new teachers want to contribute ideas and suggestions, colleagues do not always see them as being needy. A staff member dedicated to work specifically with new teachers can identify their needs and offer help. One new teacher put it this way:

> It's helpful to talk to Brenda, my mentor, about things I can't reveal to my peers or my boss. I don't always want to take peer teachers' ideas and implement them, but I don't want them to stop sharing with me because I didn't implement this one idea. I want to share with my peers, show off for my boss, but I want to get real with my mentor.

Mentors should be veteran teachers, fully aware of school and district expectations for teachers. In an elementary school in Charlotte, North Carolina, a veteran educator who left her full-time assignment on maternity leave now mentors novice teachers. The creatively funded, one-third-time position meets the needs of the school as well as those of the mentor teacher. In this model, the beginning teacher gets the benefit of collegial support as well as a dedicated staff member focused on his or her specific situation.

Solution 3: Provide teachers with tiered expectations—a gradual induction into the profession—for responsibilities involving outside duties, class assignments, and committee work. New teachers are often shocked to realize that they have more duties, more challenging classes, and more committee expectations than their more experienced peers do. The added expectations beyond regular teaching duties are often the straws that break the backs of new teachers. Gradually assigning responsibilities and duties can be a gentle way of indoctrinating new teachers. They will be more prepared, and subsequently more successful, if we present new challenges in small, incremental steps.

Solution 4: Release new teachers from regular duties so that they can grow in professional skills and acclimate to their new role as teacher. The isolation that a new teacher feels can be alleviated by periodic opportunities to network and collaborate with other educators both in and out of the school. The opportunity to observe successful colleagues in action is inexpensive, yet invaluable, professional development. Veterans often implement procedures and routines so automatically that outside the context of the classroom, they have difficulty explaining what they do. Other important reasons to release new teachers include providing additional staff development and time to research and plan lessons.

Reducing some of the stress factors can decrease the sense of being overwhelmed, a recurring lament from beginning teachers. The cost of monthly substitutes to release these teachers from assigned duties is far less than the costs of workshops, conferences, and outside consultants—not to mention the cost of replacing these undersupported new teachers.

Teaching children is hard work and requires intelligence, preparation, creativity, determination, and perseverance. Some teachers who enter the field don't have these essential qualities and consequently leave classroom teaching in search of a better career match. It is not for these teachers that I worry.

Instead, I worry about the bright, eager, and well-prepared teachers who enter the field capable of making a difference but who leave shortly after their initiation, feeling unsupported by colleagues and administrators. For these people we must change our induction practices, reexamine our new-teacher support models, and challenge one another and ourselves to be supportive colleagues. The future of teaching depends on us.

Note

[1] American Association for Employment and Education. (1998). *Teacher supply and demand in the United States: 1997 report*. Evanston, IL: Author.

Catherine M. Brighton is a graduate student at University of Virginia, Curry School of Education, Charlottesville, VA. She can be reached at 933 St. Clair Ave., Charlottesville, VA 22901 (e-mail: cmb3s@virginia.edu).

What Teachers Like (and Don't Like) About Mandated Induction Programs

Rob Danin and Margaret A. Bacon

Knowing "how things get done" and having a nurturing mentor and a supportive principal are important elements in a new teacher's success, a Colorado survey finds.

> The mentor-mentee workshops? I have to go to those. . . . They're state-mandated. They're interesting. . . . I get to meet other people, other first-year teachers.
>
> My mentor? He's saved me so many times. . . . I'd have been lost without him.
>
> I can't really remember any of the induction workshops. . . . I'm always so tired when I get to the meetings.
>
> If I need help, I always go to my mentor. . . . She's just a very caring person, very nurturing.

We know that novice teachers have a tough time surviving in our profession. In the state of Colorado, we've been doing something to help them, as these comments from first-year teachers indicate. Induction programs—organized programs designed to ease newcomers into teaching—have become the norm in many places, but the Colorado Educator Licensing Act of 1991 requires teachers who want to progress from the entry-level provisional teacher's license to a professional license to participate in a state-approved induction program. New teachers must be assigned a mentor and must have access to opportunities to enhance their classroom performance as well as to shape their own professional development. Many districts conduct monthly induction workshops to fulfill these requirements.

The induction idea makes intuitive sense, and the statistics on the dismal retention rate of our profession support the need for it. If any of our schools noted a 30 to 50 percent dropout rate, as the teaching profession does, we would be appalled. After all, other professions spend time and energy developing their beginners. Would a new physician be given a caseload of the most difficult patients with the most complex problems to solve?

Learning to teach is a developmental process that takes more than a few years of classes in educational theory and methods and a semester of student teaching. And although student teaching should give preservice students the real-life experience of conducting the day-to-day activities in a school classroom, the shock of running their own classrooms overwhelms many first-year teachers. "My student teaching was in a totally different school—much smaller, much more community-oriented—not at all like Washington. And I didn't really create my own lessons—my cooperating teacher had structured everything!" a first-year teacher explained.

A study conducted throughout the state of Colorado in 1996 examined how provisionally licensed teachers perceived the state-mandated induction program in their districts. We distributed a written survey to more than 700 new teachers. Figure 1 shows a sample of the questions.

The findings of this study, along with interviews conducted with 25 randomly selected first-year teachers, offer insights into the network of support provided to the new teacher. We learned that the monthly induction meetings with new teachers were not the vital element for them; instead, experiences that helped them adapt to school cultures and the support of a mentor teacher and an administrator saved the new teachers.

School Culture

An important goal of any induction program is to introduce new teachers to the culture of their schools (Huling-Austin, 1988). Schools that stress the importance of developing a professionally stimulating school culture celebrate the importance of collaborative interactions among staff members. These schools encourage cooperation, trust, and support within the school community (Rosenholtz, 1989).

Teachers new to a school building must quickly learn the culture and the related nuances that go along with the singular and collective

Figure 1

Excerpt from a Survey of Provisionally Licensed Teachers in Colorado on the Induction Program in Their District

Please rate, on the basis of importance and actual experience, each of these factors in your teacher induction program.

	Degree of Importance					Was this included in your induction program?	
	not important			very important			
a. planning lessons	1	2	3	4	5	Yes___	No___
b. motivating students	1	2	3	4	5	Yes___	No___
c. classroom organization	1	2	3	4	5	Yes___	No___
d. becoming familiar with subject matter	1	2	3	4	5	Yes___	No___
e. establishing realistic expectations of student behavior	1	2	3	4	5	Yes___	No___

Please respond to the following statements regarding your induction program by marking each corresponding column in the way that best reflects your own feelings and experiences.

	Occurred	Did not occur	Is this activity necessary?	Did this contribute to your success?
My mentor teacher was able to schedule time for observation and consultation.	__Yes __No	__Yes __No	__Yes __No	__Yes __No
I had opportunities to learn new instructional practices.	__Yes __No	__Yes __No	__Yes __No	__Yes __No
I learned how to conduct parent conferences.	__Yes __No	__Yes __No	__Yes __No	__Yes __No

personalities of the staff. A school's culture can have a direct effect on a first-year teacher's experience. The norms of a school can inhibit or enhance the abilities of an induction program's participants (Reiman & Edelfelt, 1990). Without a knowledge of operating norms, any staff member could feel isolated in the work environment. The same goes for knowing the community of parents and members-at-large for a particular school. A vital part of teaching is acting in a diplomatic manner with the stakeholders of the school district. Developing a team approach with both the staff and community helps ensure a teacher's success.

The culture of a building consists of not only the individuals inside its walls, but also the school's governing norms and procedural structures. In the Colorado study, 59 percent of the teachers believed that, in their individual school buildings, they were not adequately introduced to how things get done. An overwhelming majority (79 percent) of these newly hired teachers stated that their knowledge of the daily operations within the school building led to their success in the classroom. Because the building-level induction was insufficient, they had to rely on mentors and other first-year teachers, workshops, and other staff members for this information. It makes sense, then, to have building-based information be an integral part of an induction program.

In contrast, 72 percent of the teachers found that districtwide induction programs sufficiently covered the school district's requirements. Districts often use innovative methods such as bus tours to let newly hired teachers see the demographics of their school district. New teachers also usually learn about district goals and operating procedures.

Role of the Mentor

For new teachers to have productive induction experiences, their senior colleagues need to resurrect memories and feelings related to their professional beginnings. They must remember those teaching techniques that did or did not work for them in their earlier years and share them with teachers new to the profession so that they will not repeat the same mistakes (Tisher, 1979). Induction programs need to build in time for participants to share experiences.

The mentor teacher is an influential and cost-effective method for professional development for first-year teachers (Huling-Austin, 1988). Beginning teachers have expressed that their induction experience was more satisfying when their mentor was trustworthy, supportive, and willing to listen; valued confidentiality; and held similar pedagogical philosophies (Reiman & Edelfelt, 1990). Those teachers who demonstrate mentorship qualities have a tendency to reach out to others with encouragement, technical knowledge to solve classroom problems, and enthusiasm for learning new things (Rosenholtz, 1989).

The Colorado study corroborated these research findings on the importance of the mentors role in the induction process. A clear majority (88 percent) of the teachers in the Colorado study received this type of support. The teachers comments we heard highlighted the emotional and instructional assistance that mentors give to first-year teachers.

The key to the success of any induction program is the collegial relationship between the mentor and the new teacher. It makes sense to have this relationship be the central focus for any organized induction program. Although some teachers naturally assume a mentor's cloak, most mentors need training in this new role. The Colorado program calls for a minimum of two days of training, which includes information on the role and responsibilities of the mentor, coaching skills, and understanding the mentee. As one mentor in a Colorado induction program stated,

> I feel more comfortable about my role as a mentor now. I did so many things by instinct and now I have a more organized approach. The training we received was really an eye-opener for me.

The Role of Administrator Support

New teachers perceive building principals to be a vital link in their success. However, in schools that do not encourage professional growth, principals do not feel obliged to help struggling first-year teachers (or any teachers) find success (Rosenholtz, 1989).

Many building administrators who support the induction of new teachers also encourage their more experienced teachers to help in the formation of these programs (Reiman & Edelfelt, 1990). The inclusion of veteran teachers in planning the orientation of new teachers, as well as in structuring joint planning time, helps promote collaboration among those teachers and provides emotional support for the novice educator. In the Colorado study, 60 percent of new teachers thought that administrative support was crucial to their success in their first year.

Implications for New Teachers

Newly hired teachers must be willing partners in their induction programs instead of unwittingly accepting the dictates of others. For the induction process to be a worthwhile experience, new teachers must make their needs known. It is *their* professional growth at stake. Requesting a program that is tailored to their strengths and weaknesses can provide opportunities that will both enrich and remediate. In the Colorado study, new teachers often felt that the monthly meetings required in their induction programs were nothing more than repetitions of the teacher education programs they had just completed. As one mentor stated,

> I would pay close attention to whatever the new teachers say they need in terms of sessions. They know best of all. I'm too comfortable with the school and its system to see what they need sometimes.

The new teachers themselves indicated that they would like increased release time for their mentors to observe them, organized materials, a buddy system for new teachers, and an in-school teacher induction program. Over time, these types of experiences are increasing.

Implications for Mentors

A mentorship agreement is based on how well the mentor and the mentee match in such factors as commitment, accessibility, and teaching assignments. In addition, mentors need a keen understanding that their role is vital to both the mentee's and the program's success. Mentors must fully comprehend their role as guide and advocate for the teacher in their charge. Their ability to be supportive is central to the induction program.

Many teachers attribute their initial professional achievements to their mentor's help in solving problems. They also appreciate their mentor's ability to offer encouragement. In the Colorado study, teachers who viewed their relationship with their mentor in a positive way generally gave higher marks to the overall quality of their induction programs. The reverse occurred when teachers were less satisfied with their relationship with their mentor.

Prospective mentors need to judge whether they have the personal and the professional qualities to do the job. Mentors need the ability to be supportive and to demonstrate care and concern. They should express a sincere interest in taking on the role. Mentors should understand the needs of the mentee and be willing to listen. And they must be trustworthy and value confidentiality.

And we must not overlook the benefits of mentoring for the continued professional development of the mentors themselves. One mentor discussed the effects of the induction program on her own growth:

> I see so much of myself in her. And that has been one of the interesting lessons I have learned as a mentor. It has been interesting to see how far I have come and that doesn't mean I know it all or am a better teacher than she is.
>
> I have both lost and gained insights over the last 14 years and sometimes I wish I were as flexible, as innocent as she is. She'll try anything and tries to explain everything. I have learned to economize in time and frustration, but I have lost the spontaneity I used to treasure. Maybe working as a mentor has helped me realize that, and now I will recapture it.

In his classic study of the sociology of teaching, Lortie (1975) states, "For most teachers, learning by experience has been a matter of learning alone, an exercise in unguided trial and error." As we approach an era in which we will need vast numbers of new teachers, shouldn't we think about creating environments that will help these teachers, as well as their students, continue to grow and learn?

References

Huling-Austin, L. (1988, April). *A synthesis of research on teacher induction programs and practices*. Paper presented at the annual meeting of the American Educational Research Association, New Orleans, LA.

Lortie, D. (1975). *Schoolteacher*. Chicago: University of Chicago Press.

Reiman, A. J., & Edelfelt, R. A. (1990). *School-based mentoring programs. Untangling the tensions between theory and practice*. (Tech. Rep. No. SP 032 904). Raleigh: North Carolina State University.

Rosenholtz, S. J. (1989). *Teachers' workplace*. White Plains, NY: Longman.

Tisher, R. P. (1979, January). *Teacher induction: An aspect of the education and professional development of teachers*. Paper presented at the National Invitational Conference, Austin, TX.

Rob Danin (e-mail: rdanin@mail.uccs.edu) is an Instructor and **Margaret A. Bacon** (e-mail: mbacon@mail.uccs.edu) is an Associate Professor at the University of Colorado at Colorado Springs, School of Education, 1420 Austin Bluffs Parkway, P.O. Box 7150, Colorado Springs, CO 80933-7150.

The Best Lessons: Learning to Teach in a Supportive Context

Debra M. Sullivan

A beginning teacher reflects on how supportive administrators create an atmosphere for professional growth.

On our way to a conference for new teachers in independent elementary schools, two of my first-year colleagues and I reflected on our first six weeks at the Chestnut Hill School. We spent much of a two-hour car ride from Boston to Little Compton, Rhode Island, talking about our supportive Head of School, reflecting on our Assistant Head's role as the new-faculty mentor, and considering the impact of such administrative guidance on our first year of teaching. Although each of us taught a different grade and faced a variety of professional challenges, we all drew strength from the collection of resources put in place to support us.

After spending three days at the conference, however, with beginning teachers from all over New England, we realized that we should not take our positive experience for granted. Many new teachers from other schools felt deprived of administrative support and envied the concept of our first-year mentoring program. Grappling with all of their anxieties as new teachers, our counterparts felt alone and inadequate. My colleagues and I drove home from the conference grateful to have begun teaching in a supportive environment.

A Community of Learners

In an affluent suburb just outside Boston, the Chestnut Hill School is a small, independent school that serves 175 students from preschool through 6th grade. Coming from a wide range of cultural and socioeconomic backgrounds, our students benefit from a progressive, developmental, multicultural curriculum and a strong sense of school community. One class is taught by two full-time teachers at each grade level. I coteach the youngest class in the school, which is a half-day program with a full-day option, for 16 three-year-olds. This is my first full-time teaching position since I completed my master's degree in early childhood education last spring.

When I started teaching here, I sensed that I had stumbled into a circle of educators who would not only make me love teaching but also push me to be a better teacher. Dealing with parents, designing curriculum, developing management skills, and creating a multicultural classroom have challenged me throughout the year, but a carefully constructed network of personal and professional resources has supported my work. This network has scaffolded my learning as a new teacher in at least four important ways: the guidance of a mentor, an administration familiar with the needs of my students, a sense of shared ownership in my growth as a teacher, and a reliable network of administrative and peer support.

Mentoring New Teachers

As the cornerstone of the New Faculty Mentoring Program, Assistant Head of School Roslyn Raish meets individually with new faculty members each week. In this confidential setting, I can explore ideas about my teaching, reflect on how particular lessons did or did not succeed, and brainstorm what I might do differently in the future. Most important, our conversations are opportunities for me to reflect on my students and to ask questions or to raise concerns that I might have about their academic, social, or emotional growth.

I depend on Roz's thoughtful feedback, whether I am searching for guidance with an upcoming challenge or mulling over a past event that I wish I had handled better. By sharing relevant stories from her own teaching experience or by suggesting connections that I may have overlooked, she sheds light on the issues that I raise and helps me put problems in perspective. Our meetings are tutorials in the art of practicing reflective teaching. I look forward to our mentoring sessions as time to stop and think about the meaning of my work.

Roz is a source of tangible support because she shares her knowledge of educational theory and practice so readily. I knew exactly where to turn when a parent called with concerns about handling the topic of race in a preschool classroom, when I ran out of strategies to ease a student's separation anxiety, and when I needed a second opinion on a bibliography for a presentation to parents and other faculty. In addition to offering me advice, she refers me to resources both inside and outside the school, identifying the books, the people, or the organizations that may give me insight on a problem. Through our conversations, Roz empowers me to find my own solutions. To help me develop professional problem solving skills and self-confidence, Roz leads me to the right questions as often as she leads me to the right answers.

I value this mentoring relationship, however, not only because it is practical but also because it is personal. Roz knows me well enough to effectively support my teaching. She has greatly enriched the quality of my first year of teaching and has played a central role in the formation of my identity as a teacher.

Connecting with Students

Visitors to the Chestnut Hill School often remark on the fact that Head of School Susan C. Bryant knows every student. Her frequent visits to classrooms and her interactions with the broader school community benefit the students, and her hands-on approach provides valuable instructional opportunities for new teachers. I learn from watching her. When Sue addressed my class about an unsafe behavior, for example, she taught me how to handle similar behaviors in the future. When she reads stories or answers students' questions at lower-school community meetings, she models effective ways of engaging students and responding to their concerns.

Equally important, Sue's connection to the students informs her guidance of their teachers. She meets with each teaching team biweekly to learn more about each team's classroom and to offer administrative support. She often opens the meetings with such inquiries as, "Whom are you worried about?" or "How can I help you teach better?" I suspect that most administrators do not regularly ask their new teachers these questions, much less listen to the answers. These scheduled meetings are ongoing forums for program reflection; in them, we gather insights on emerging curriculum questions or student concerns. Suggestions are helpful because they are often based not only on experience, but also on personal knowledge of the students and the teachers.

In a similar way, Roz's frequent involvement with the students benefits my teaching. Her formal observation of one of my lessons early in the year gave me feedback about simple management techniques that I can use in the classroom, such as reminding the students to raise their hands when the excitement level in the group builds, and new ideas for enriching the curriculum, such as using additional literature with my flannel-board literacy activity.

Late in the year, Roz videotaped one of my lessons. After reviewing the video on my own and then discussing it with her, I recognized some opportunities that I had missed to extend my students' learning, as well as some previously unnoticed social dynamics that were operating in the class.

But the informal, daily observations that my mentors make of my students are even more useful than their formal observations of me; they are a constant reminder that teaching is a dynamic exchange between student and teacher that can never be evaluated or improved on in isolation. My mentors model the essence of child-centered education. Their guidance is a product of the time they take to know me and my students. I believe that the investment that my administrators make in supporting faculty is the fullest expression of their commitment to serving students.

The Journey Toward Experience

When administrators communicate a commitment to reflective and child-centered teaching by how they spend their time, they communicate a faith in new teachers. Big gestures, such as the institution of a mentoring program, and little gestures, such as frequent special recognition for new faculty, send messages of support and appreciation. My administrators encourage me to take pride in my growing skills and abilities that, although less practiced, are no less valued than the contributions of my more experienced colleagues.

Through demonstrating faith in my abilities, the faculty and the administration of the Chestnut Hill School create a supportive atmosphere in which I am comfortable asking for help when I need it and am not afraid to admit mistakes. When I pulled Sue out of a meeting to help me manage a group of 3-year-olds run amok, she did not see me as a failure—she saw the situation as an inevitable challenge that occurs when teaching young children. When I inadvertently angered a parent, Sue trusted my judgment and suggested follow-up steps that successfully restored the relationship. Quick to offer stories of her own foibles as a new teacher or a reassuring hug when something falls apart, Sue conveys the message that making mistakes and growing from them are an expected part of learning to teach.

The administration shares ownership of my professional growth by supporting the development of my skills and the discovery of my voice as a teacher. The partnership between the faculty and the administrators is reflected in my school's annual evaluation process. At the end of October, Sue asks each faculty member to list his or her professional goals, and in early spring, she asks us to complete a detailed self-assessment. We used my prepared reflections during my evaluation meeting to share thoughts and feedback on my teaching. Rather than emphasize what I have yet to accomplish as a new teacher, Sue used these reflections to validate the things that I do well and to suggest improvements in the areas that I perceive as weaknesses.

For example, she suggested that I augment my assessment efforts by keeping notes on index cards. This technique has helped me document my students' progress more systematically and better understand their individual needs. The administration recognizes that professional development is a joint endeavor between faculty and administration, and it offers me support and encouragement for achieving my goals. Beyond the boundaries of this meeting, the administration continually facilitates my learning in a highly individualized way by conveying appreciation of the personal qualities and experiences that uniquely affect my teaching.

Support Networks

In addition to direct administrative guidance, a wide range of other school supports has enhanced my work this year. For example, I have received valuable peer support from my coteacher, who provides a steady source of ideas and feedback within our classroom. This team approach permeates the entire school.

Substantial professional development opportunities inside and outside the school also enrich my teaching. The school provides the funding and the time to attend relevant workshops and conferences. Internal opportunities to extend my learning include monthly multicultural forums that address the complex issues of diversity and educational equity. We also have on-site staff development days devoted such topics as instructional technology and behavior management. At the start of the year, I found such informational resources as a new-faculty orientation and a regional conference for beginning teachers helpful. The faculty's participation in the professional development program maintains a flow of new ideas and energy in the school.

I also appreciate having a cohort of four other new teachers with whom I share the exciting—and sometimes overwhelming—experience of first-year teaching. Through our own initiative and the efforts our school makes to bring us together, we offer one another moral support and occasionally exchange resources and curriculum ideas at similar grade levels. As we struggle with the common fears and frustrations of new teachers, such as navigating the norms of school culture or writing a first set of reports, this informal peer network provides the care and the understanding that only new teachers can offer one another.

With few exceptions, the supports that I have used this year are not special privileges of my status as a new teacher. I will continue to receive professional support at the Chestnut Hill School because the administration promotes growth and learning at all levels. The most significant ways that my school supports new teachers are really the same ways that it supports all teachers.

The Best Lesson

I have learned that the most important thing that I can teach my students is that they are known and loved. On that crucial foundation all meaningful growth and learning take place. The support system for new teachers teaches me the same lesson—and it gives me opportunities to develop my skills in a setting that is both challenging and nurturing.

I know from my experience this year that effectively supporting new teachers is as intricate and personal a process as teaching itself. It does not happen by accident, and it does not happen without the active and thoughtful participation of good administrators who are, first and foremost, good teachers. If I have learned to teach my own students half as well as the administrators have taught me, then this year has been a success.

Debra M. Sullivan is a preschool teacher at the Chestnut Hill School, 428 Hammond St., Chestnut Hill, MA 02467 (e-mail: dsullivan@tchs.org).

Helping New Teachers Keep the Light in Their Eyes

Beth Hurst and Ginny Reding

What can new teachers learn from veterans who still love to teach? Continue to learn, choose material and techniques that interest you, and, above all, enjoy your students.

We were on a mission. We set out to find teachers who still love to teach even after years in the classroom and who still find teaching an enjoyable and fulfilling career. In a profession in which pressure, stress, and little thanks come with the territory, it is easy for teachers—veterans and novices—to get discouraged and want to quit. We know; we are teachers ourselves.

We reasoned that one way to help new teachers maintain their enthusiasm is to find out how experienced teachers renew their original passion for teaching. Today, stimulating our students is becoming increasingly difficult. We believe that to increase student interest and motivation, teachers must themselves show enthusiasm for teaching and learning.

Much publicity has been dedicated to the subject of teacher burnout. Identified causes include work overload, low pay, lack of appreciation, poor preparation, inadequate facilities, undesirable student behavior, struggles with self-confidence, lack of time management and organizational skills, little peer support, excessive paperwork, and professional isolation. The list goes on. We know the causes of burnout; we want a cure.

In our search for answers, we interviewed more than 70 teachers who still love to teach. We talked with real teachers who have faced and dealt with the problems that all teachers face and continue to get up each

---

Authors' note: This article is based on *Keeping the Light in Your Eyes: A Guide for Helping Teachers Discover, Remember, Relive, and Rediscover the Joy of Teaching* by Beth Hurst and Ginny Reding (Scottsdale, AZ: Holcomb Hathaway, 1999).

morning ready and eager to enter their classrooms. We searched for these teachers' secrets of success.

As we talked with dozens of teachers around the country, we found a theme running through their answers to the question, What keeps the light in your eyes? Teachers may talk for hours about what they do and how they feel, but in the final analysis, what keeps the light in their eyes reduces to three things.

First, teachers themselves love to learn and find that the more they learn, the more they want to learn. Knowledge is in itself a reward. Second, teachers have learned to bring their own likes and interests into their teaching. They look for ways to make learning meaningful not only to their students, but to themselves as well. And last, and as they will tell you, most important, teachers love their students. As they see their students succeed, and see the light of understanding in their eyes, they know that what they do is all worthwhile. And teachers are proud to stand among the ranks of those who change lives—they know that they have made a difference.

Enjoying Learning

Most of the teachers we interviewed mentioned that learning is one of the main ingredients that keep them going. We teachers love to learn. That's why we became teachers. To us, learning is not something we do just at school; learning takes place in our everyday lives—as an old Chinese saying goes, in our chopping wood and carrying water. We learn as we tend our gardens, shop for groceries, or read the newspaper. All of life is a learning process. Whether we are discovering better ways of handling relationships, new ways of solving problems, or more effective ways of doing our jobs, we are learning something.

Part of our job as a teacher is to show our students how we learn in all situations. By teaching our students how to ask questions and how to find their own answers, we teach them how to become lifelong learners. It is important that we be active members in the learning process in our classrooms. We need to let our students see that we are learning with them, that learning takes place everywhere, that learning is forever.

We teachers are in the business of igniting in our students that excitement. One way is by creating opportunities for our own learning. If we are not involved in the process ourselves, our own light is dimmed.

High school teacher Bob Brady shares some of his own philosophy about learning.

> One reason we become teachers is that we like learning. I have some flexibility in what I teach and how I teach it. I might design a lesson on a theme about something I want to learn more about. I make it an excuse for learning.
>
> For example, this year I required my students to memorize a poem by Goethe, the great German poet. I used this opportunity to do some personal research on his life. I tried to connect this guy with what my students were learning in 11th and 12th grade history and literature. I learned a lot in doing this, and some of my students got involved in researching Goethe as well. I have done the same with Martin Luther. On the 450th anniversary of his death, I created a unit. Students got involved in the story of Luther's life and his contributions, and together we learned a great deal about him. . . .
>
> I have found that you have to look for opportunities to keep learning for your own self-satisfaction. Just because you have a credential doesn't mean that you've stopped learning.

Elementary teacher Lori Elliott has a fresh outlook on new trends in education:

> I overheard a teacher at a conference say, "Some teachers say that trends in education run in cycles so they quit paying attention to them, but I learn something each time they come around." I really liked that. I am always on the lookout for good ideas, and I feel that I can learn from anyone or anything. . . . The more I learn, the more I want to learn. The more I learn, the more I want to change and get better.
>
> I've had people ask me how I know the material I teach with my units. I just tell them that I am researching the information right along with my students. When I tell my kids we are going to learn about what it was like to be a cowboy in the old West, I mean literally that *we* are going to learn about it. *We* go to the library together; *we* check out books; *we* get on the Internet; *we* read the encyclopedias. It's that constant learning that I love about teaching.

Our students can be sources of learning for us if we let them. Ralph Waldo Emerson said, "Every man I meet is my superior in some way. In that, I learn of him." We are all teachers, and we are all students. One way to make teaching more meaningful is to allow ourselves to become learners with and from our students.

Making Learning Meaningful

The fulfilled teachers we talked with have learned to look for ways to make learning meaningful for themselves. As educators, we have been trained to focus on the student. We are told to define his needs, identify her problems, discern the educational strategies that benefit them most.

Although focusing on our students is important, we have learned that as we teach, we need to look at ourselves as well. If we enjoy what we do and are excited about a subject, if we are interested in an idea or a concept, we will be more successful at drawing enthusiasm from our students. Dale Carnegie,[1] who learned from successful leaders in the field of business, quoted a man as saying,

> A man rarely succeeds at anything unless he has fun doing it. I have known men who succeeded because they had a rip-roaring good time conducting their business. Later, I saw those men begin to work at the job. It grew dull. They lost all joy in it, and they failed.

Teachers can learn a great deal from this observation. When we are having a good time, when we make learning meaningful for us, we will be successful, fulfilled teachers.

Veteran teacher Schyrlet Cameron, a 1997 recipient of the Presidential Award for Excellence in Science and Mathematics Teaching, likes designing projects and enjoys writing grants, not only because they benefit her students, but also because they keep teaching interesting for her:

> I always have a lot of projects going all the time, both at school and at home. . . . And the kids have projects too. We recently started a mail system in our school, and my students named our room Project Plaza. . . .
>
> The project I was working on when I won the Presidential Award was . . . the Case of the Missing Millionaire. The students were given information about a crime that had been committed. The classroom was cleared and the students reenacted the crime scene. The local sheriff came to talk to the "suspects." The students had to study the facts to solve the case. We even visited the county court house and met with the circuit judge. Back at school we reenacted the court case, videotaping the whole thing. We even had jurors who decided the verdict. The students and I both had a ball with this. . . .
>
> These projects give me something to think about. I can be driving down the road, and I will be thinking about the next project I am going to do. I need to be creating and doing. . . . And that's what I like about being a teacher. I'm right there and I am actively involved. And I am trying to get the kids involved with me. I try to get their minds working, and

> I tell them that anything is possible. I tell them to let their minds wander. If they want to do a project, I tell them to think of the wildest thing they could do. I want them to do anything other than writing a report. That was so boring for me as a student. And reading their reports is boring for me as a teacher. But with projects I learn so much, too.
>
> One of the things I get out of writing grants is the personal feeling of knowing that I can do it. I am a terrible writer. I struggle with every word. It takes me a long time to write a grant. I see it as a self-help thing. They are my projects. I get a great sense of satisfaction from the accomplishment of completing one. If a grant is not accepted . . . I read the reviews and suggestions, rewrite it, and submit it the next year.

We all need to realize that only we can change the environment in our classrooms. It is our responsibility to make our classes what we want them to be. If we have become complacent in our teaching, then we need to ask ourselves, What can I do today that will make this a meaningful and fulfilling day? Instead of focusing only on meeting curricular objectives and doing paperwork, we can change our perspective: How can we teach what we need to teach in ways that will be interesting and relevant to us? We can make teaching more meaningful by adding our own personalities, styles, and interests. The best things that we as teachers can do for our students are to enjoy being teachers and to find ways to make teaching meaningful for us.

Before an airplane takes off, flight attendants instruct parents that in an emergency, they should put on their own air masks first. If parents pass out from lack of oxygen, they cannot help their children. The same can be said for teachers. If we burn out because of a lack of passion, we cannot effectively help our students. We need to be aware of what makes learning meaningful for us because as we make it work for us, it will work for our students as well.

Enjoying Our Students

Perhaps the number one reason that most of us become teachers is to make a difference in the lives of our students. We remain in the profession because of the difference our students make in our lives. The glow of that "light of understanding" when they finally grasp something that we have been trying to teach is what gives us fulfillment. From prospective teachers to retired teachers, all have an energy, a light, that keeps finding its way into our eyes when we talk about learning and kids.

When prospective educators are asked why they want to become teachers, they often respond by saying, "I just love kids." Although there is much more to being a good teacher than enjoying children, that love is still at the heart of good teaching. We can love kids and not love teaching, but we can't love teaching and not love kids. Fulfilled teachers love their subject, and they love their students.

Tracey Hankins, an elementary teacher nominated for teacher of the year in her school district, says that students are at the heart of her love for teaching.

> These kids become such an important part of my life. They are the reason I get up every day to go to work and face the many challenges we teachers face. As I reflect back on my years of teaching, I feel as though my students are like my own children. It is so hard to turn loose of them to let them go on to the next grade level.
>
> Kids can say things in passing that you'll cherish and never forget. One year I wore to school a sweatshirt with the logo MSTA, Missouri State Teachers Association. One of my students, Diana Kaercher, asked me what MSTA stood for. Being the experienced teacher I was, I turned her question around and asked her, "What do you think it stands for?" Diana replied, "Most Special Teacher Alive!" I had just received the compliment of my life. Another teacher in our district heard the story and shared it with the state MSTA office. The next year, MSTA used "Most Special Teacher Alive" on all their promotional items. What an honor that was for me.
>
> Just as Diana had made an impact on my life that day with just a simple comment, I realized that I am making an impact on each and every child's life in my classroom by the way I act and the things I say. And just as her comment had a larger impact on other teachers across our state, I never know what larger impact my words will have. It is my goal to touch as many children as I can. The little compliments we give each other really do make a difference!

As the old saying goes, "Nothing succeeds like success." Nowhere is that idea more true than in the classroom. Success snowballs. One student happens onto a little success, and all the others want to jump on the bandwagon. Good teachers take advantage of that. They plant seeds, water, feed, and nurture, and one day success blossoms.

When teachers stay focused on the success of our students, we taste victory ourselves. When apathy begins to take root, or when the reality of student achievement seems hopeless, we should tune in on the success of our students. If we provide an atmosphere in which success is the only thing that can grow well, not only will our students blossom, but we will be energized as well.

Enthusiasm Leads to Good Teaching

As we interviewed teachers from around the country to find out what keeps them enthusiastic about teaching, we heard the same basic story: "Teaching has meaning to me." And we found something else interesting. Although our focus was not to look for "good" teachers but to interview teachers who still enjoy teaching, we discovered a strong relationship between the two. It was almost as though we had handpicked people from a teachers' hall of fame. Each person in his or her own way had something extraordinary to say, something profound, something of significance. We met award winners, grant writers, creative geniuses, and teachers who tenaciously persisted in giving their best. One of the secrets of being a good teacher is to enjoy teaching. And one way to continue to enjoy teaching is to work to make teaching meaningful for ourselves.

New teachers may feel so overwhelmed with the demands of the job that they focus on survival, not on self-fulfillment. They may not even see the need to be concerned about anything beyond the demands of the classroom at this time in their lives. But for their sake—and that of their students and schools—we need to guide new teachers to an understanding that they must take care of themselves. In so doing, they will make themselves into more productive and caring teachers.

In our efforts to support new teachers, we need to remember to encourage them to hold on tightly to their original passion for teaching. And those among us who still love to teach can light the way by being positive role models and by showing new teachers how we find our own ways to keep teaching meaningful. As retired teacher Mary Wright told us, "You catch the spirit of teaching, the spirit of learning, and the spirit of caring; they all go together." What an encouraging commentary this is—and good advice for all new teachers.

Note

[1] Carnegie, D. (1936). *How to win friends and influence people*. New York: Simon & Schuster, p. 98.

Beth Hurst is Assistant Professor of Reading, Department of Reading and Special Education, Southwest Missouri State University, Springfield, MO 65804 (e-mail: BethHurst@mail.smsu.edu). **Ginny Reding** is an adjunct instructor at Southwest Missouri State University, Springfield, MO 65803 (e-mail: var590t@mail.smsu.edu

Ask Not What Your School Can Do for You, But What You Can Do for You

Lisa Renard

Despite rocky beginnings and a lack of initial support, new teachers who take a proactive approach can make their early professional years positive ones.

Angie Rodriquez knew before she was hired that she was a candidate for a position opening mid-way through the school year. One morning, she was shocked out of bed by a phone call, only to find that it was not about the usual substitute teaching job. Instead, it was from the resigning teacher.

"Angie," she said, "we need to get together and arrange some turnover."

Angie sat, uncomprehending. "But I haven't been offered the job," she said.

"That's funny," the amused voice at the other end of the line replied. "The principal announced at yesterday's faculty meeting that you are my replacement."

That's how Ms. Rodriquez found out that she was hired. The principal never did call her. Neither did his secretary. Tired of waiting, and curious beyond belief, Angie finally went to his office and asked about the situation. He casually told her that the personnel office needed to have her paperwork completed that afternoon. As she drove to the personnel office, Angie wondered how long he had intended to let her wait before telling her.

The school did not assign Angie to an experienced mentor. In fact, administrators never officially introduced her to the faculty because she started the school year after the official "welcome back" faculty meeting.

It seemed to suffice that many of her colleagues knew her as a substitute.

No new-hire packet was available to Angie. No one asked whether she had received a faculty handbook, and no one offered her one. Indeed, she never met with her administrator or department chair after being hired, except for receiving a cursory greeting in the hall.

Angie's administrator did arrange for a week of transition with the resigning teacher. When Angie arrived, however, the teacher asked her to take over the class immediately and then disappeared into a separate office to work on her own resignation details. Angie's turnover consisted of receiving some information on the students, a copy of the first-semester course outline, and some student-work samples. Hired on a Friday and expected to have a full-semester plan submitted by the following Monday, Angie didn't find the school's curriculum guide until three weeks later.

No one offered to teach Angie how to use the school's computer grading system or intranet mail system; perhaps her colleagues figured that she had learned what she needed to know when she was a substitute. The personnel office told Angie that her administrator would discuss her salary and benefits. Her administrator told her that the personnel office would take care of that. She didn't receive a paycheck until the end of her first quarter of teaching. When she inquired about the delay, Angie was told that there were people who hadn't been paid for much longer than that.

The Reality

Angie Rodriquez's induction into the teaching profession sounds awful, even ridiculous. Although I haven't used her real name here, her story is true to the detail—and it happened within the past three years. It tells an important tale about new-teacher support.

The same year Angie was hired, her school sent two experienced teachers to a workshop on creating a teacher mentoring program. The school was about to join the current trend toward supporting new teachers through formal, organized programs and policies. However, the year following this training, new teachers still had no mentors and no induction program.

School districts accross the country now advocate reform of new-teacher support in an attempt to reduce high migration and attrition rates during the critical first years. The truth, however, is that even with support programs cropping up nationwide, we have not seen a prevalence of effective programs in schools. The National Center for Education Statistics (Ingersoll & Alsalam, 1997) concedes that even while a majority of schools offer formal programs for new teachers, only a minority of teachers agree that the assistance is adequate or effective.

A World of Challenges

Few teachers relate positive experiences about their professional induction. I recently asked colleagues about their perceptions and experiences as new teachers. I was told that new teachers—both those new to the profession and those new to a district or a school—face a world of challenges and disadvantages. Experienced teachers shuddered to remember their induction, and the newer teachers told of survival despite, rather than because of, the support that they received.

Individual anecdotes of new-teacher stress are backed by statistics on teacher migration and attrition. In 1994–95, the majority of teachers migrating to different schools did so within the first three years (Whitener, Gruber, Lynch, Tingos, & Fondelier, 1997). According to the same report, the highest percentage of those leaving teaching as a profession did so during the same early years. Among teachers choosing to leave during the first three years, more than half did so before finishing their first year.

What causes attrition during the early years? Despite recent trends to institute formal support programs, many educators perceive that neophytes get the short end of the stick. This is what prompted Halford (1998) to remind us that teaching is sometimes referred to as "the profession that eats its young" (p. 33). Too often, new-teacher needs are ignored when they should be addressed.

My quest to learn about teachers' perceptions revealed that brand-spanking-new, just-out-of-the-wrapper teachers are often assigned to the behavior-problem classes, the low-achiever classes, and the most challenging grade level in the school. They are perceived as frequently finding themselves in the classrooms that nobody else wanted with the equipment left over after experienced teachers ransacked the room.

Some new teachers don't even get a classroom or equipment of their own. They must add to their learning curve the interesting challenge of pushing a cart around the school in search of other teachers' classrooms, where other teachers' bulletin boards are decorated with other classes' information. They must organize and plan out of broom-closet-sized offices, if they are granted an office at all.

Wong and Wong, in their popular book for new teachers, *The First Days of School* (1998), concede that being a new teacher is unreasonably demanding. Teaching, they say, is the only career in which one must immediately fulfill a complete set of duties while trying to determine what those duties are and how to do them. The pressure that new teachers feel is real, as put succinctly by Schempp, Sparkes, and Templin in *Identity and Induction* (1999): "Teachers have little choice but to meet the required demands, for failure to do so means risking the loss of their job" (p. 147). New teachers, they say, often find this pressure "crushing."

What to Do? What to Do?

Angie Rodriquez had a rocky beginning. She found herself confronted with challenging circumstances at the beginning of a new and daunting career. Though she did inherit a fine classroom and some of the higher-level classes from the resigning teacher, she felt the awful isolation and uncertainty of being a new teacher without adequate support.

I should tell you now that at Angie's year-end evaluation, she received the highest possible rating. Her evaluator sat across the table from her and told her that she was an "educational leader." This praise came after just one semester of teaching. Angie not only survived her rocky beginnings, but she also thrived as a new teacher in a school with no organized induction program or support system.

Angie Rodriquez did experience frustration, anger, and disappointment from time to time. She met obstacles and made mistakes. But when people didn't hand answers to her, she went looking for them. Angie knew that one of the most important factors in her success was her ability to be proactive.

Being Proactive

In *The Seven Habits of Highly Effective People* (1989), Covey says that being proactive "means that as human beings, we are responsible for our own lives" (p. 71). "It is inspiring," says Covey, "to realize that in choosing our response to circumstance, we powerfully affect our circumstance" (p. 86). Covey is discussing the basic principle that when life does not go the way that it should, truly effective people do not throw their hands in the air, cry "victim," and give up or move on. People who apply Covey's idea of being proactive to their teaching careers become educational leaders.

When I read articles about new teachers, I am confronted with such issues as, "How can we better support new teachers?" That's nice. But why don't I ever read about "The top 10 ways new teachers can help themselves," or "How to make your first years the best years"? The focus of our efforts to help new teachers seems to weigh too heavily on the schools; we forget to encourage new teachers with practical steps to help themselves.

In this age of abbreviated teacher-training programs, alternative certification, and emergency teacher placements, a growing number of teachers have the potential of arriving in classrooms feeling inadequately prepared. Instead of arming themselves with the additional resources that they will need to be successful and sane during those first years, too many stand isolated, wondering bitterly where their welcoming committee could be.

This sounds harsh, I know. The truth is that districts and schools do need to do more to ensure new-teacher success (and therefore retention). Analysis of teacher perceptions reveals that new-teacher support programs still fail to hit the mark in terms of effectively helping new teachers (Ingersoll & Alsalam, 1997). However, this is only part of the truth. The other part is that new teachers need to be resourceful, tenacious, and self-motivated to equip themselves with essential knowledge and skills.

What to Do! What to Do!

New teachers can do some concrete things to prepare themselves with the knowledge and skills to excel during those first few years:

- Find out how to use the programs and equipment that you need on a regular basis by asking colleagues specific questions. You won't look dumb if you pay attention and do it for yourself the next time.
- Scour your room and department for resources that will give you an idea of what you are expected to do. Get your hands on a faculty hand-

book. Seek out that curriculum guide. Sure, it should have been given to you. But if it wasn't, find it.

- If you weren't assigned a specific colleague mentor, recruit an unofficial one.

- Don't be afraid to say "I don't know." It seems to give senior colleagues a certain satisfaction to hear newbies say those three words. They are the experts and are often glad to share wisdom and resources. Note that I did not say "whine and complain to others." That elicits a whole different reaction, which is to be labeled "needy" and "ineffective."

- On your own, seek out information about teaching. If you feel inadequate in a particular area, don't expect the school to bring you up to speed. Find books, Internet resources, anything that will improve your knowledge and skills. Expect to spend time on your education beyond the walls of the university.

- Take classes—even tiny, one-unit, minicourses. Keep educating yourself. So your school hasn't offered you the inservice program that you feel that you need. Find a comparable course on your own and go for it.

- Equip yourself with knowledge about current research-based, best-known teaching and assessment practices. *Motivation & Learning* (Rogers, Graham, & Ludington, 1998) provides important ideas for your classroom. You'll also want to read about multiple intelligences and brain-compatible learning. Books by Eric Jensen or Renate and Geoffrey Caine will start you out well.

- Read resources intended for new teachers. *The First Days of School* (Wong & Wong, 1998) is an excellent beginning. Take care when choosing to be certain that the resources advocate current, theoretically sound practices. Avoid the myriad new-teacher resources that promote outdated and unsound practices, such as shaming students as a form of discipline or planning classes solely for teacher convenience.

- Join professional organizations and subscribe to journals. Doing this keeps you informed and helps alleviate your feelings of isolation.

- Choose your friends wisely. If the group in the lounge whines, complains, and gossips, eat elsewhere. Seek colleagues who seem happy, enthusiastic, and professional.

Being hardworking, smart, resourceful, and willing to seek assistance—these are the things that will make you successful during those first years of teaching.

Fear of Being New

Being proactive is not the same as being pushy. Being proactive is recognizing our ability and obligation to make things happen in our own lives (Covey, 1989, p. 75). New teachers who allow their probationary period to paralyze them are not on the right track. Being new is neither a sin nor an offense warranting termination. Novices can be tactful in seeking assistance. When you do that well, no one will fault you for being new.

For all its tribulations, Angie Rodriquez considered her first year a huge success. She discovered that she was pretty good at teaching. She sought and found the help and answers that she needed. She was tenacious in arming herself for success, not waiting on her school to do it for her. Being proactive paid off.

Success by Sheer Will

In theory, new-teacher programs are terrific. I can't wait to see more of them, more completely integrated, in more school districts. But until the reality of new-teacher support programs matches the theory, new teachers must still rely on themselves to a great extent. If you want to be the best teacher that you can be, if you want to be an educational leader in your own right—ask not what your school can do for you, but what you can do for yourself. Make your first year a great one by sheer will, if nothing else.

References

Covey, S. (1989). *The seven habits of highly effective people*. New York: Simon & Schuster.

Halford, J. M. (1998, February). Easing the way for new teachers. *Educational Leadership*, 55(5), 33–36.

Ingersoll, R., & Alsalam, N. (1997). *Teacher professionalization and teacher commitment: A multilevel analysis*. NCES 97-069. Washington, DC: U.S. Department of Education.

Rogers, S., Graham, S., & Ludington, J. (1998). *Motivation & learning*. Evergreen, CO: Peak Learning Systems.

Schempp, P., Sparkes, A., & Templin, T. (1999). Identity and induction: Establishing the self in the first years of teaching. In R. Lipka, & T. Brinthaupt

(Eds.), *The role of self in teacher development.* Albany, NY: State University of New York Press.

Whitener, S., Gruber, K., Lynch, H., Tingos, K., & Fondelier, S. (1997). Characteristics of stayers, movers, and leavers: Results from the teacher followup survey: 1994-1995. NCES 97-450. Washington, DC: U.S. Department of Education.

Wong, H., & Wong, R. (1998). *The first days of school.* Mountain View, CA: Harry K. Wong Publications.

Lisa Renard is an English teacher. She created and maintains The New Teacher Page at http://www.new-teacher.com in support of new and aspiring educators. She can be reached at 3 Rosehaven St., Stafford, VA 22554.

Index

About the Editor

Marge Scherer is Editor of ASCD's *Educational Leadership*. A former classroom teacher and department chair, she has received national awards for her writing on education topics. A recent interview, "The Discipline of Hope: A Conversation with Herb Kohl" (*Educational Leadership*, September 1998), was a finalist in the 1998 EdPress Distinguished Achievement Awards competition. You may reach Marge at el@ascd.org.

Related ASCD Resources: Mentoring

Audiotapes

Coaching for Intelligence Under Block Scheduling
How to Mentor in the Midst of Change by Cheryl Granade Sullivan

Print Products

Educators Supporting Educators: A Guide to Organizing School Support Teams by Margery B. Ginsberg, Joseph F. Johnson Jr., and Cerylle A. Moffett
How to Help Beginning Teachers Succeed by Stephen P. Gordon
How to Mentor in the Midst of Change by Cheryl Granade Sullivan
Supporting New Teachers, *Educational Leadership*, Vol. 56, No. 8, May 1999

Videotapes

Mentoring the New Teacher
Mentoring to Improve Schools

For additional resources, visit us on the World Wide Web (http://www.ascd.org), send an e-mail message to member@ascd.org, call the ASCD Service Center (1-800-933-ASCD or 703-578-9600, then press 2), send a fax to 703-575-5400, or write to Information Services, ASCD, 1703 N. Beauregard St., Alexandria, VA 22311-1714 USA.